RETIRE SPIRITUAL PILGRIMAGE:

Stories, Scripture, & Practices

for the Journey

by

R. JACK HANSEN &
JERRY P. HAAS

WHAT READERS ARE SAYING ABOUT THIS BOOK

This book goes beyond what most of us regard as the critical aspects of retirement, namely finances, to explore the emotional and spiritual needs of retirees. The book is so compelling and relevant because it includes the verbatim insights, opinions, and real life experiences of retirees. This book is not only for every retiree or pre-retiree to understand the realities that retirement will bring to them, but this is a great book for group study and discussion. I see this book as being a powerful instrument to use with small groups or large seminars for those who are retiring or in retirement.

Jack Tatar (Founder, People Tested Media)

This engaging read has awakened a desire for creativity in my retired life of seven years. Had I read the suggestions for practicing prayerful discernment as I prepared for retirement, I may have stimulated this desire and need for renewing life at this time in my journey.

Sr. Joan Stoffel (Retired Educator)

"Retirement as Spiritual Pilgrimage: Stories, Scripture & Practices" for the Journey is a must-read for every one preparing for retirement as well as those who have already entered into retirement. Feedback gained from a study of numerous retired individuals provide a plethora of helpful insights in both how to truly enjoy the opportunities inherent in the retirement phase of life as well as potential pitfalls to be avoided. As a Life Coach, I recommend this book as a helpful resource for making your retirement the best phase of your life as you follow the helpful guidelines outlined by Hansen and Haas.

Don Graybill (Navigator Staff)

This book, offers a thoughtful, spiritual approach to a question: what about retirement? Asserting that this life-stage passage is a significant opportunity, not just a change in role, Jack Hansen and Jerry Haas provide spiritual insights and questions relating to the

2

personal aspects of the transition: meaning, friendships, intellectual and spiritual growth, health, identity, and hope for the future. The book takes the reader far beyond the "gold-watch party" way of thinking about entering retirement. As a former professional counselor, I see this as a much needed resource for working with people in transition toward retirement. As a recent retiree, I see it as an affirmation that retirement can indeed be challenging, gratifying, and meaningful!

Skip Gebhart (Retired Executive and Counselor)

Those who put their

strength in you

are truly happy:

pilgrimage is in their hearts.

Psalms 84:5 (Common English

Bible)

Cover photograph: Photo by Dee Anne Bostic (www.deeannebostic.com) as she walked El Camino de Compostela. Crossing over the Pyrenees in France, just before reaching Spain, she had been hiking all day in the rain and wind gusts up to 50 mph. Suddenly the wind subsided and the rain began to clear. She took this photo, a sacred moment on a long, adventuresome pilgrimage of some 500 miles. Used by permission.

Acknowledgments: We gratefully acknowledge the enormous contribution made to this work by the men and women who have shared their retirement stories in writing, as well as those who have reviewed and provided very helpful comments on the manuscript. We are also indebted to Kathleen Stephens for her excellent editing of the book.

Contents

Introduction

Our adult lives are marked by a variety of important transitions—everything from getting a driver's license to leaving home to marriage, having children, and losing a loved one. Prayers and rituals generally mark some transitions in life (baptisms, weddings, and funerals). Various cultures and religious traditions add to the list of celebrations (First Communion—Roman Catholic; Quinceañera—Hispanic; Sixtieth Birthday—Korean). Each includes a gathering of friends and family and an offering of wise words, hopes, and blessings as a way of honoring life's changes.

When a person retires, there may be a party; but often there is little recognition that this is a significant adult life transition with a whole set of unique opportunities and challenges. And the spiritual dimension of this passage is rarely recognized, either as an occasion for public prayer and guidance or in our own thinking and planning for this new phase of life. Retiring from one's career is most often seen as a purely private, secular, and financial passage, rather than a transition fraught with personal meaning and profound implications for one's family and friends.

Our interest in the personal dimensions of life beyond full-time work dates back almost a decade. One of us (Jack) was beginning this transition as a participant in the Academy for Spiritual Formation and the other (Jerry) observing this experience as the Director of the Academy while anticipating his own retirement in a few years. We were surprised then (and still are today) by the contrast between abundant financial advice on retirement and the virtual absence of guidance on the personal topics (relationships, sense of meaning and purpose, opportunities for intellectual and spiritual growth, and the like). These matters are critical to our sense of well-being in every phase of life, including retirement. Feeling that an understanding of these more personal areas of retirement would benefit those of us approaching and living this stage of life, we interviewed retired men and women about their own experiences and wrote the book *Shaping a Life of Significance for Retirement* about the key findings. [1] The interviews clearly showed that we face a common set of personal transitions as we prepare for and enter retirement, are afforded several unique opportunities in this phase of life, and meet several personal challenges as we continue to age.

In this book, we seek to bring spiritual insight to each of these personal dimensions of retirement. We offer one or two first-person accounts, a reflection on a relevant Scripture passage, and a suggested spiritual practice for each transition (chapters 2–4), opportunity (chapters 5–8), and challenge (chapters 9–12) that are identified in our earlier book. We have now interviewed seventy-five retired women and men at length, representing a broad range of ethnic backgrounds, life experiences, and financial circumstances. We have also interacted with well over a thousand retirees in seminar settings. These interactions have confirmed that the personal elements of retirement we described in our earlier book and elaborate upon in this one are quite common. They have also given us an appreciation of the rich variety of each retiree's unique experiences. Most of all, however, our own experiences of retirement have been enriched as we have walked on the sacred ground of personal stories of loss, doubt, and new beginnings that have been shared with us. We were struck by the spiritual search that many intuited: Who am I? What's my purpose in life now? How much time do I have left on this earth, and how will I cope with whatever suffering may come my way? Have I come to grips with my mortality or do I still think I'm going to live forever? We trust that your journey into and through retirement will also be enriched as you encounter some of these stories, ponder the Scripture with us, and incorporate some of the suggested spiritual practices in this unique phase of life.

What is at stake, after all, is not just surviving retirement, but thriving in this new phase of life. Retirement often means entering the third phase of life, and like every liminal state, it's a time of vulnerability and openness, possibility and danger. Benedictine Sister Joan Chittister accurately identified the challenge when at age seventy she wrote, "The task of this period of life . . . is to come alive in ways I have never been alive before."[2] This book (along with our earlier one) is offered to help you navigate this exciting journey.

How to Use This Book

This book can be used as a stand-alone resource, or in combination with *Shaping a Life of Significance for Retirement*, in three ways. The first is as a guide for personal reflection. Every chapter includes questions for deeper thought. We suggest that individuals write responses to these questions in a journal, and then look back at them from time to time. From experience we know that when writing one's thoughts, changes in thinking occur, and deeper responses emerge unexpectedly.

This book is also suitable as a guide for a small-group study. Groups of six to eight people are optimum for this experience, but one could also imagine smaller and slightly larger groups. Such small group sessions facilitate in-depth sharing. Because of the vulnerability involved, participants agree to a covenant of full-time participation. Newcomers are not allowed after the first session to secure the confidentiality of the group. Sessions are generally ninety minutes long and may best be held in the home of one of the members. Appendix A of this book provides guidelines for such a group and a suggested outline of a typical session addressing a personal dimension of retirement.

Thirdly, this resource is suitable for an adult Sunday school class. Regardless of size, Sunday morning classes are often open-ended, with people coming and going on a regular basis. Confidentiality may be limited and so is time. Forty-five minutes is often all that's available with people coming late and leaving early (to join the choir or other responsibilities). Appendix B is an outline for a session of this type.

In either the small group or adult Sunday school setting, constraints on the length of the series may dictate that the leader choose a subset of the topics covered in this book. We recommend that consideration be given to the life circumstances of the participants. For example, if the majority of the participants are approaching and in the first few years of retirement, the first eight chapters may be of most interest. And if the participants are further along in their retirement journey, some of the later chapters may address current concerns for them. Our own experience in conducting one-day seminars is that there is broad interest in the whole range of topics covered.

Recognizing that most Christians do not currently receive the blessing of their pastor or congregation when they retire, we include some suggestions as to how a new retiree might be honored in worship (see Appendix C). With or without such a ritual, church leaders may wish to give this book to the layperson or pastor making such a transition.

1 Beginning the Journey

As children most of us have to be taught the importance of going from point A to point B without a lot of dawdling in between. Children love to find all kinds of alternatives to the straight-line path. Only later do we gain the concentration to walk through life without distractions. Gradually through schooling and through the hard knocks of life, we are taught to focus on our goals in order to achieve as much as we possibly can.

And yet, such a singular focus on the final destination can cause us to miss much of the richness that exists along the way. The interstate highway may be the quickest way to get somewhere, but most of the journey is not memorable. The topography of the landscape may go unnoticed in our high-speed travel. Because of our pace, we may bypass local restaurants in favor of chains, and the food tastes the same whether the exit is in New York, Tennessee, Texas, or California. If only the final destination is important, we may arrive no different than when we left; and our senses may be too numb to appreciate the uniqueness of this place we have hurried to get to.

We think it helpful to experience retirement as a particular type of journey, a pilgrimage. The pilgrimage journey begins by slowing down. Disengaging the compulsion to arrive as quickly as possible, we begin to pay attention to the world around us, and eventually to our own feelings. We see, we smell, we listen, we taste, we feel, and eventually, we notice a Presence we had not expected in our lives. As the sages have said, God often hides things by putting them close to us, and a pilgrimage is all about slowing down so we can see.

For many people the longing for retirement is the longing to reclaim such a spiritual perspective on life. Viewing retirement as a spiritual pilgrimage is not a one-time decision, however. It is easy to get caught up in the same anxious striving as before. This reality suggests the importance of preparing for retirement by developing practices to help us pay more attention to God, to ourselves, and to others. In this chapter we consider a personal account of the journey into retirement and how a spiritual orientation enriches each step. We then look at a late-in-life calling to such a journey in Scripture. And finally we explore the spiritual practice of telling our stories as an aid in embarking on this journey.

Experience of Retirees

Sharon (*retired bishop in a Protestant denomination*)

> I grew up in a family where travel was valued as a learning tool. From the time I was in third or fourth grade until I graduated from high school, my mother, father, brother, and I had a two-week vacation somewhere in the United States each summer.

> Late in the fall each year, my parents would decide where the next summer's vacation travel would take us. My father would then order up Conoco Oil Company trip maps and other materials that would give us information about best roads to travel, places to stop and see along the way, and good hotels, motels, and cabins that might fit our price range.

> I remember well winter nights at home in Michigan with maps and brochures scattered on the floor as our family learned about and planned for the coming summer's trip to California, New York, the Grand Canyon, or some other destination. The planning was part of the trip. The actual trip was both a new experience and recognition of all the things we'd learned during our winter preparations.

> Once we set out, we began each day with family devotions, and I realize in retrospect how important this simple step was in helping us be attentive to the unique experiences and people God had for us in that day. We traveled to places we'd

never been before, trusting those maps, trusting all we'd learned, and as kids trusting our mom and dad to protect and shelter us wherever we were. When we got home, we were not quite the same as when we left. We knew more about the world, we'd met people unlike ourselves and visited places unlike Michigan, and of course we had new ideas about where the next journey might take us.

For me, the journey into retirement has had some parallels to those childhood experiences. There was the planning: deciding an appropriate time to begin, gathering resources (financial, property, etc.), animated discussions with colleagues and family about what we might encounter, and the assurance of shared caring and support with loved ones and God. Like the trips of long ago, there have been times when the road we anticipated was changed or not available. Sometimes events around us have necessitated developing new plans. And as in the childhood trips, daily orienting myself each day to God's purpose and pace has allowed me to be attuned to that purpose, including interruptions and detours. Living in a new community and interacting with people not like those I've previously known has changed my perspective and commitments.

For Discussion and Reflection

1. Sharon describes the months of planning that went into the summer vacations that her family took when she was a child. In what ways is this analogy a good one for retirement preparation?

2. She also describes the importance of maps and guidebooks for her family. We are probably familiar with the idea of financial planning for retirement. However, what other areas of life would be enriched with thought and attention as you prepare for this new phase of life? You might give attention to questions such as the following: How do I build new friendships or sustain existing ones?

How do I structure each day? What do I invest myself in? Should I continue working part time in an area related to my career or some new area of interest? Should I consider relocation?

3. Finally, Sharon shares that her family included a time of devotions before traveling. How might you prepare spiritually for this next phase called retirement?

Witness of Scripture: A Late-in-life Calling

Read the record of God's extraordinary call of Abram: "Now the Lord said to Abram, 'Go from your country and your kindred . . . ' So Abram went . . . [He] was *seventy-five years old* when he departed . . . " (Gen. 12:1–4, italics added). The story of God's people begins here, with the call of Abram (whose name would later be changed to Abraham). It is a call to "go from your country and your kindred" and travel to a far-off land that would later be known as Israel.

Abram's story suggests that life with God involves making a journey, which may or may not involve geographical relocation. The Bible is full of stories about people responding to a call from God and venturing forth on faith into a new identity and purpose. From this perspective, retirement may be viewed as part of the faith journey. This journey can sometimes seem like dying, as we leave the old and familiar and enter something new. Yet our faith proclaims that such dying is never the end of the story. And when we die to ourselves, Christ raises us up to new life. In times of transition, we may be tempted to wallow in our grief or push back those feelings entirely. When we name our losses and offer them to Christ, we open ourselves to new growth and possibilities. Think back to the major transitions in your life and see if this isn't so.

Scripture says that Abram was seventy-five years old, which serves to remind us that it is never too late to begin, or begin anew, the spiritual journey. Preparing for or entering retirement may be exactly the right time to respond to God's invitation to begin again. What would it mean for you to consider retirement as a spiritual pilgrimage? What promise might there be for you as you begin or continue this part of your life? What challenge or challenges do you anticipate?

For Discussion and Reflection

1. At this stage of his life (seventy-five years old) Abraham was called to a journey that was deeply spiritual, a journey of faith. What might it mean for us to consider the years beyond the careers to which we have devoted ourselves as a faith journey?

Spiritual Practice: Telling Your Story

The urge to tell your story is sometimes strong when making the transition from full-time work to whatever follows. Feelings and experiences are vivid, and we need to find a way to process them with a friend, a family member, or a counselor or coach. After years spent in shaping a career, however, it takes more than an initial venting to share the story completely or in a way that is helpful.

The need to tell one's story is one of the reasons we recommend keeping a journal as a regular spiritual practice during this transition. Spending time every day recording your thoughts and feelings for no one to see but you is enormously therapeutic. Perhaps the greatest benefit is that you become aware of your thoughts and feelings. Because transitions are often stressful, such awareness reduces the inclination to blast away in anger or withdraw in hurt when things go wrong. It may even help us catch a glimpse of God at work in friends, family, and the timing of our retirement.

Becoming aware is the first step in telling your story. And to some extent, retiring as a spiritual pilgrimage means helping you tell your story in the context of God's story of transformation and hope.[1] We'll explore more of this in future chapters, but for now, here are a series of prompts or questions to help you get started. Your story is important and needs to be told. Your story can help others know they are not alone. And your story can reveal the grace of God at work in your life.

First thoughts

- What comes to mind when you hear the word *retirement*? What thoughts and feelings does that word evoke?
- When did you begin thinking that one day you would retire? How did you respond to that notion?
- Whether you initiated the retirement process or someone else did (boss, spouse, etc.), how has this been or how might this be a learning experience for you? Can you imagine it as an invitation to grow closer to family, friends, and even God?

The event

- As the day of your retirement came nearer, what thoughts and feelings do you recall? (Or, if not yet retired, what thoughts and feelings do you anticipate?)
- Did you have a retirement party? Was it something you initiated or others initiated on your behalf? Was it helpful or painful, easy or difficult? (Again, if your retirement is in the future, what do you anticipate such an event might be like?)
- What was it like immediately after you retired? Were you tired, relieved, sad, or happy?
- What if anything surprised you during this transition?

Further reflections

- What did your parents do well in retirement? What can you learn from their experience, or the experience of others who made this transition?
- What were the key relationships in your working life, and what feelings do you have about these relationships now that you're retired? (Or if still working, what are the key relationships and how do you anticipate feeling about them as you retire?)
- How has God been present to you in this transition? Was there a particular prayer that helped you to stay centered during this time?

2 Living with Meaning in a Smaller World

In her book *Little Pieces of Light ...: Darkness and Personal Growth*, Joyce Rupp observes that "darkness can break into our inner world when we experience the natural patterns of adult growth, such as midlife, retirement, and other aging processes." [1] This was the experience of many of the men and women we interviewed as they entered the smaller world of influence, authority, or recognition of retirement. These individuals expressed feelings of loss, sadness, or lack of purpose or direction as their world became smaller in one or more of these ways.

In this chapter we listen to a retired teacher's experience of entering into the smaller world of retirement. Then, we consider passages of Scripture that describe individuals as they move to a smaller world and are separated from that which is familiar or has given them meaning or sense of purpose. And lastly, we introduce the spiritual practice of letting go of things so that we can see the full promise and potential in what may seem a smaller world of retirement.

Experience of Retirees

Brenda *(secondary school teacher prior to her retirement)*

> For twenty-four years I had seen the faces of teenagers every day and heard their cries for help or kindness or recognition. I was even able to teach them a few things about our English language on some days, though not nearly as often as I planned and hoped for. Life got in the way for them and for me most of the time. On bad days, nothing went right. On good days, there was magic in that classroom.
>
> For years I planned my retirement, for I knew the day would come when I would hear God's voice

saying, "Now is the time to retire." My planning was all about me and my filling my days with intentionality and purpose for God's kingdom here on earth. And then it hit me: what about my students? Who would love them as much as I did? Who would listen to them when their mother's new husband wanted them out of the house in favor of the new baby? Who would nurture the shyest girl or boy? Who would call their parents to say something good about their sons or daughters? Who would scold them when they needed it?

My questions kept coming because I truly cared for my students, admittedly some more than others. Some tried their hardest to keep me from reaching them, and they succeeded. I could not and did not save the world, but I tried to do my part to make it a better place and to be a good teacher every day.

So I was torn. What to do? Teaching well hardly gave me time for anything else in my life except going home so tired I could hardly get a decent meal on the table for my husband. Then it dawned on me that fatigue was taking its toll on me in every area of life. I had to come to grips with the fact that God had already said that it was time to leave my students. New questions came from God: Do you think too highly of yourself? Are you the only one who will take care of them? Do you just need to be in control? Is your concern really about them or are you feeling empty? Do you not remember that I will be going into retirement with you?

I played out these scenes in my head for months. I asked the hard questions over and over again. Then I remembered that I really had made plans to retire all along, but I had not owned them. Once I took ownership of those plans and trusted God's promises to be with me, it became easier to let go.

I'm on this side of retirement now, and my leaving hardly made a ripple in the ocean of education. New teachers have taken my place beautifully, the students are still coming and going, and so am I. It was a troublesome and bumpy journey to retire, but I thank God for it every day. God has gifted me in more ways than I could ever have imagined. My planning ahead has led me to new adventures that I never dreamed were out there for me. To God be the glory.

For Discussion and Reflection

1. Individuals we interviewed described the transition to a smaller world in a variety of ways. Brenda anticipates the loss of influence on the lives of young people as the focus of her grief. Other individuals interviewed focused on the loss of authority, recognition, or workplace environment. As you think about your own work life and transition into retirement, what losses come to mind? What dimensions of this smaller world are or will be most problematical for you?

2. What consolation did Brenda experience that helped her to accept her retirement? How was God present to her through this journey? What seemed to surprise her the most?

3. One of the consolations retirees sometimes experience is a sense of legacy—passing on to others something of value. How would you describe the legacy that Brenda is leaving behind as she moves into retirement? What legacy do you want to leave?

Witness of Scripture: Transition to a Smaller World

The Bible offers numerous examples of individuals who went from a larger to a smaller world of influence, authority, recognition, or status. Surprisingly enough, it's often in this smaller world that God speaks most clearly. Of course, these transitions were not associated with retirement as we think of it today, but they nevertheless offer insight as we think about our lives and God's presence throughout our lifelong journey, whether we're working or retired.

Take for example the apostle Paul, a Jewish leader and a Roman citizen, who forsook this larger world of influence and authority to follow Jesus. Read Galatians 1:16–21, which describes the years of relative solitude following Paul's conversion, spent in Arabia and Damascus and additional years in Syria and Cilicia. This time preceded his assuming a place of prominence in the early church. Some of us may feel like we've been knocked off our horse as Paul was (Acts 9:1–9). Yet it is in this downward movement that we may encounter God most significantly.

Exodus 2:11–4:17 provides another example—the period of Moses's life when he fled the Egyptian capital for the desert. Because of a crime he had committed, Moses went from the privilege and prestige of a king's son in the Egyptian capital to the life of a fugitive in a remote region. The Scripture makes clear that it was here in this smaller world of the desert that Moses first encountered God. It is almost as if Moses had to get away from the distractions and expectations of the larger world to hear God clearly and to see God work uniquely.

Finally, consider Mary's encounter with an angel in Luke 1:26–38 and 2:1–7. The point is not that Mary has gone from a larger to a smaller world. It is instead an indication of how God can work. While the gospel writer refers to the larger world of Caesar Augustus and Pontius Pilate, he makes it clear that God's most important work is in this smaller world of everyday life. God is at work, but not always in the places that we had imagined.

For Discussion and Reflection

1. In each of these examples, a smaller world provided the context for God to do a new thing. What other examples can you think of from Scripture or from your own life experience? What new thing do you feel God might be doing in your life as you enter the smaller world of retirement?

Spiritual Practice: Letting Go

Letting go may not seem like a spiritual practice. After all, we all have to let go, sometimes reluctantly and sometimes with pleasure. Yet letting go can often be the way in which we open ourselves to the next thing that God has in store for us. As Scripture says, "Those who want to save their life will lose it, and those who lose their life for my sake will save it" (Luke 9:24).

In her book *How Can I Let Go If I Don't Know I'm Holding On*, Linda Douty provides helpful insights on both the why and the how of the spiritual practice of letting go. Of particular relevance is her discussion of letting go of roles we have had earlier in life but have now left (or need to leave) behind. These roles were both necessary and legitimate at one time. However, we must leave these behind in order to, in her words, "use the gifts we have been given to pursue the passionate interests that compel us to be all that we are created to be" in this new phase of life. [2]

Linda suggests three steps in the process. First, make a list of your losses. That may seem simple, but probe a little deeper. You may miss having a project to do and even miss those deadlines you used to dread. You may miss working on the project with Joe, who always thought outside the box and forced you to think in new ways. You may miss the satisfaction of being a part of a team, the feeling that you've accomplished something. What else do you miss?

The second step is feeling the pain of the loss. Some of us have trained ourselves to stay away from our feelings. That training may have helped us be task-centered, problem-solving professionals. When we slow down, feelings are more likely to surface and we may become uncomfortable. It's okay to take some time with this and let the feelings come.

When we retire, we may be tempted to throw ourselves into busy work to avoid the–feelings of loss, emptiness, and lack of direction. In fact, one of us [Jerry] did just that early in retirement, volunteering for several boards and committees as well as teaching several classes and coordinating various projects. Both of us, and many we have interviewed, have a whole lot to unpack from all those years of work. Linda's advice is to take time to experience some of the feelings that surface by identifying our losses. Here again, keeping a journal can be a helpful tool in the process.

Once you've named the losses and given yourself time to feel the pain, the third step is asking God to help you resolve your feelings. If there is anger or resentment, ask God to help you begin to forgive. Forgiveness is a process; it takes time. You may want to write out your feelings directed at the person or situation that caused your hurt. Here again is a place where keeping a journal can be a valuable practice. (If you write a letter to someone, you may want to set it aside or burn it rather than mail it and regret what you did later on.) Many people find it helpful to write a prayer or a letter to God; God knows and welcomes all of our feelings, including feelings of betrayal. If you have unexpressed gratitude, now is the time to acknowledge something beautiful in your heart and mind. That may be a letter you want to send.

It is helpful to keep in mind throughout the process of letting go that you are on a journey toward the next good thing in life. Or, paraphrasing the words of Loretta Marshall, "When I am on what seems to be a set of dead ends and winding paths, openness to the surprises of God's Spirit can move me from lostness to a highway of grace."[3]

3 Retirement and Family Relationships

During the season of Advent we may say something to the effect that Christmas is not a Hallmark card. In this expression is the recognition that our expectations about a future event (e.g., family together to celebrate a festive occasion) may differ substantially from the reality (time spent bickering, criticizing, or in other unhelpful ways).

Men and women approaching and in the early stages of retirement make a similar observation about family relationships. This period of life offers the potential for enriching family relationships by virtue of additional discretion in time and schedule. But the reality in some cases is not as attractive as anticipated. Differing expectations for retirement can draw spouses apart rather than together. Differences in perspectives on parenting or any one of a range of other topics can cause tension between parents and adult children. Grandparents may feel imposed upon or taken for granted if there is too much expected by way of childcare. And some of our siblings may not seem all that interested in rebuilding a relationship that has been fallow for years.

In this chapter we explore the potential impacts of the move from full-time work to the next stage of life on these most important family relationships. We first reflect on the experiences of two retirees who faced significant challenges early in retirement and discovered the importance of listening closely to other family members in these circumstances. Then we examine a passage of Scripture where there is an obvious failure to listen to other family members. And finally we explore attentive listening in these relationships as a spiritual practice. Family relationships are inherently complex, and there are no silver bullets to make them perfect in any phase of life. Still, we suggest that the practice of listening attentively, together with forgiveness when it is needed, may be of real benefit in these relationships.

Experience of Retirees

Carol *(retired university executive)*

At age fifty-eight, I had worked my way to the top—or at least the seventh floor of the building—and stood lost in reverie looking out at the beautiful trees in the fall. Without fanfare, a voice spoke to me saying, *Leave your job.* God was calling me to retire and embark on another leg of my faith journey. The next spring I took early retirement and went home to our house in the woods to see what God had in store for me. Suddenly I had time for family and friends, as well as a more intimate relationship with God. For the first time in many years, I was able to engage in the spiritual practices of reading Scripture, centering prayer, and journaling each morning in an unhurried manner. This regular pattern has kept me grounded with both God and family. Because of my daily communion with God, I am better able to conduct my retirement life. That life has focused primarily on our large extended family.

Ours is a second marriage with five children from both marriages and three grandchildren who have become "ours." Initially in retirement, I was unaccustomed to thinking of family as a source of friendship and entertainment, but as the first year of retirement ended, I realized that family had become our primary source for both. Because we retired early, we have had the time and energy to see our children and grandchildren often. We take vacations together—sometimes with the parents and sometimes without them; we frequently visit our children who live out of state; we go to school plays, concerts, and all manner of grade school and now high school sporting events. And as the grandchildren have grown older, we have taken the opportunity to expose them to the professional theaters, museums, and orchestra that we have available in our area.

When we retired we had four parents alive and healthy. We visited them, took trips with them, and as they grew more infirm, we had the time to serve and be with them in their final days. All along the way was that still small divine voice encouraging me to be kind, to be patient, and to be a role model for our children. Without my daily spiritual practice, I could not have been God's faithful servant, for I am not patient and usually prefer to read a book rather than care for the sick. I am often reminded of 1 Timothy 5:8, "If anyone does not provide for his relatives . . . he has disowned the faith and is worse than an unbeliever" (RSV).

Finally, retirement has created a stronger bond between my husband and me. While working we certainly knew that we loved each other, but we were often too tired or busy to remember to cultivate our sincere love. Now it is not only our desire but also our responsibility to care for each other. We take the time to really listen to one another, allowing us to feel each other's pain and happiness, and to know and love the joys and honors as well as the hurts and sorrows that make up each of our daily lives. This has given us a sound and lasting relationship that now extends beyond our own lives to include our entire family.

Larry (*retired urban planner and city executive*)

When my wife and I retired, we had been married for forty-five years. Yet, since retirement we have experienced two events that have challenged us as never before, both as a couple and as individuals. The first was a direct hit by Hurricane Ivan. Our newly remodeled home was damaged to the point that we had to live in the cramped quarters of our camping trailer for several months while we completely rebuilt our

26

house and tried to figure out what we should do next. Should we wait for this home to be rebuilt and move back in, despite its proximity to the waterfront and risk of damage by any future storm? Should we look for another property in a more sheltered location? Should we perhaps leave the area altogether for some part of the United States that never experiences hurricanes? We spent long hours talking and seeking to listen deeply to one another, as well as to friends who were also experiencing the trauma imposed by a natural disaster. In the end, we decided that the course of action for us was relocation to a less exposed home nearby.

About the same time, our oldest daughter (living on another coast) sank into a deep depression and needed our support and encouragement to help her deal with this illness. After almost two years, thankfully, she was able to return to work and to raising her family. This was a different but also difficult challenge for us. In this circumstance also we found it important to communicate deeply about how we together could be helpful in this situation, with complexities of which we were only partially aware.

These two challenges not only taught us anew the importance of really communicating with one another. It has also renewed our faith journey together and our regular participation in a church community. We have developed deep friendships with several couples in our congregation and also have become involved in areas of ministry that now are an important part of our lives.

An additional blessing of the last few years has been that our younger daughter and her family have relocated to our community and are active in the same church as we are. This has given us the opportunity to engage with her, her husband, and our grandson in new and wonderful ways.

For Discussion and Reflection

1. Both Carol and Larry identify significant post-retirement events that have affected their family relationships (death of parents, displacement by a hurricane, illness of an adult child). What helped them get through these challenges in a positive way?

2. What significant, challenging events or issues might impact your family as you move into retirement?

3. While you may be able to anticipate some circumstances affecting your family relationships, others will come as a surprise. What might you consider doing to help foster better family relationships regardless of circumstances?

Witness of Scripture: Listening (or Not) in a Family

Genesis 42:1–46:4 is an account of listening and forgiving in a particularly dysfunctional family. Ten of Joseph's brothers had years earlier sold him into slavery. Motivated by jealousy, they had taken this step over the objections of Joseph's eldest brother, Reuben. Now, in a time of deep remorse, fear, and need (Gen. 42:21–22), Reuben laments their failure to listen to Joseph's pleas and his brothers' failure to listen to his admonition to not harm Joseph. They do not yet know that the Egyptian official before whom they are standing is the same brother they sold into slavery many years before.

In the Joseph story, we see how a family found a way to move past their history of envy, deception, and failure to listen to one another to discover forgiveness and new life. The story illustrates how one person's capacity to move beyond the cycle of jealousy and retribution affects everyone in that family. Their story is a dramatic tale with a surprising ending.

Not every family is as dysfunctional as this one. Yet, every family and every family relationship can change for the better with more honesty, intimacy, and loving kindness. As you retire, you will

28

experience what for many is a major transition in life, with the potential for significant impact on your family relationships. You may find yourself wanting to grow closer to your loved ones. At the same time you may want to distance yourself from the daily challenges and the discord that is part of family life. Conversation and negotiation are often needed, and so is a healthy dose of humility and repentance.

For Discussion and Reflection

1. What are some lessons for family relationships in the later stages of life that you draw from the events recounted in Genesis 42–46? For example, what allowed Joseph to get beyond resentment and bitterness toward his brothers?

2. Certainly one theme in this account, and indeed in the Bible as a whole, related to relationships is reconciliation. Are you aware of a need for reconciliation in a relationship that has been troubled? Since reconciliation is a two-way street, what small steps might you begin to take to move toward resolution?

3. The story of Joseph and his brothers reminds us that sibling relationships are often conflicted. In retirement, these conflicts sometimes come to the fore as sisters and brothers have more time to relate to each other. A helpful reflection on sibling relationships in later life is *Sisters and Brothers All These Years* by Lillian S. Hawthorne.[1] Do you have a sibling with whom you would like to have a closer relationship in retirement? What practical steps on your part might facilitate this being a reality?

Listening Attentively as a Spiritual Practice

Most people agree that healthy relationships begin with good listening, and listening is particularly important as we seek to understand one another's expectations for retirement. Good listening is both a skill and an attitude. It is not easy to listen well, and the core of the problem is within our souls. How do we develop the capacity and the desire to listen well to another person, especially when that person is a member of our family whom we want to listen to us?

In the book of James it is written, "let everyone be quick to listen, slow to speak, slow to anger" (1:19). The words *listen, listens,* and *listening* appear numerous times in the Bible, sometimes with reference to God and sometimes to one another. Together these passages point to a reality that we know and experience all too often. Talking or getting angry in reaction to what a loved one says is easy, but listening closely, hearing a loved one while not reacting, is challenging.

One way to start becoming a better listener is to take some time in quiet every day if you can to pray for a loved one. Consider this process: begin by sitting in a comfortable position and breathing deeply, remembering how the word for breath and the word for spirit are the same in the Bible. Take five or six deep breaths and gradually bring your loved one to mind. Notice the feelings you have as you think of him or her. If you are angry, let yourself experience that feeling and then let it go (as we practiced in chapter 2). Get in touch with what you want from your loved one. It's not uncommon to want to fix someone or withdraw in the face of conflict. Continue to breathe deeply in a relaxed manner as these thoughts and feelings come to you. When you are ready, ask yourself, how does God see this person? As you ask that question, new insights may come to mind regarding past actions, failures, or motivations. Perhaps now you are ready to pray this or a similar prayer:

> *God, help me to listen more fully to _____today. Help me to let go of my anxieties and my desire to make _____ over in my image, rather than in your image. Give me an open and wise heart to hear my loved one for who [he or she] is and is becoming. In the name of the One who listens so well to our innermost thoughts and feelings. Amen.*

Preparing *spiritually* to listen is only one part of the process. As mentioned, good listening is also a skill. Asking the right questions to elicit the real feelings and expectations of the other is also a skill. Such simple questions as how do you feel about . . . ? or what's it look like from your perspective? offer tremendous potential for drawing out those intentions and expectations that a loved one may not have fully articulated or appreciated.

Putting attentive listening into our daily lives has the potential to communicate respect and love in a way that few other activities do. Or in the terms used for the title of a popular book growing out of NPR's Story Corps project, "Listening Is an Act of Love."[2]

4 Retirement and Friendships

The term *good friend* can mean everything from a person we have interacted with only superficially to someone with whom we have a relationship of deep devotion and caring. In our first book, *Shaping a Life of Significance for Retirement*, we discovered that deeper friendships are important among retired men and women. Two priorities in friendship emerged in our conversations: first, sustaining and deepening our most important, long-term friendships; and second, reaching out and embracing new friends.

With these priorities in mind, we first look at the experiences in friendship of two retirees. We see in their words some of the challenges and rewards of friendship in this phase of life. We then seek to learn about being a friend from one familiar scriptural example. Finally, we look at the spiritual practices of attentiveness and self-disclosure as ways to open doors to new friendships and deepen existing ones.

Experience of Retirees

Buzz *(retired pastor)*

> It struck me soon after I retired that I had few close friends . . . hardly any. I wonder how much of the loss has to do with retired pastors no longer being the center of attention. No matter how successful ministers might be on the job, there is an element of on-stage recognition that can be captivating from day one in the pulpit. We experience weekly affirmation throughout our active ministries. Retired clergy may feel unneeded and unimportant by not being able to tend to a flock, but the greater loss may be that congregational connection and compassion that goes with being a pastor.

So, in retirement most of us preachers learn quickly that friendships don't automatically come to us now. We have to make a concerted effort to befriend people. Some of us are not good at establishing a relationship or instigating first-time meetings. I think I need clergy friends now more than ever. Pastors have been through and dealt with stuff with which I resonate, but it's not always easy to connect with them now that I no longer am actively pastoring a congregation.

What is it about a colleague, active or retired, that keeps us from giving them a call to get together? It could be a long-standing, not-so-subtle, competitive spirit—and the inevitable comparing of past churches—that makes us reluctant to connect with a former colleague. There might also be dread that she/he will detect that our theology isn't all that sound.

What I want is a connection that goes beyond mere chitchat. In other words, I want to share our dreams, deeper concerns, fears, and joys. I know the only way to draw close to a colleague is to risk making the first move. It is never easy. Most seem to assume I have a hidden agenda. When they say, "I'll get back to you," I wonder if it conveys they might have a better offer, or that they need to think it over.

A year into my retirement, I chose to initiate a dozen calls to others because frankly I was lonely, and I wanted to befriend some preachers. The first colleague seemed eager to meet and promised to check his calendar and get back to me. He never did. The second person acted suspicious and finally claimed he was too busy. Three of them met with me once, but I never heard from them again. Then I hit pay dirt. An active pastor agreed to have lunch. Since then, we have met monthly for four years and have drawn exceptionally close. So, I went after another unsuspecting parson, and we developed a similar relationship.

A colleague I've known for over forty years always accepts my invitations to go for coffee or lunch about once a month, but he has never called to invite me. What's that about? I don't have the nerve to ask him why he has not contacted me. I might learn he is not all that keen about our meetings.

Pat *(retired nurse and social worker, Jack's wife)*

After twenty-three years of being the one who always said goodbye to friends leaving, my husband and I became the ones looking in the rearview mirror with tears in our eyes. And then we got on the five-year plan with the moving company and relocated four times in fifteen years. Cross-country moves offered new adventures but lots of challenges. And this last move into the place of our retirement is no exception.

Our first major move brought the challenge of saying goodbye to long-term friends and leaving behind a personal history spanning early marriage, raising a daughter, and becoming empty nesters. We were sent forth equipped with photo albums, cards, gifts, exchanges of love and appreciation, and hugs and well wishes. Each of the moves began with goodbyes celebrating shared memories and being launched toward a new community for us to embrace.

With some friends we never say goodbye. They are the ones we pick up where we left off no matter the distance or length of time between visits. Those are my soul friends who are part of my life history. This diaspora of soul friends is a blessed gift and how these friendships happen is often a mystery. But within this mystery is effort and intentionality.

Finding friends begins with showing up and paying attention. Church has been the typical location, but by no means the exclusive place I have shown up. The hardest thing I have ever done is to go to a ladies function not knowing a soul. I fortified myself with prayer that God would show me a woman who looked more scared and lonely than I. When my smile was returned with a spoken greeting, it became a high holy moment.

In those early days in a new location, just getting out of the house can be a huge effort. Saying hello and stopping for a quick chat can reveal the friend God has put in our path. It takes effort to be aware of what is in front of us. Impromptu cups of tea in my messy kitchen can lead to the initial stage of being a friend. Retirement and a new location give an extra margin of time available for those God encounters.

Making a friend is like exercising a spiritual discipline. Following the Spirit's nudging, we take the initiative to follow up with a call and an invitation for lunch, coffee, or whatever allows you to spend time together. Find something you are interested in, and ask one of your new acquaintances to go along.

We are all people with lots of different facets to our personalities and interests. At times I need a friend who is light and upbeat, who makes me laugh. Then there is the friend who challenges me intellectually, or the one who is an artist and helps me see beauty. No one friend is going to be all things to me all the time. The process of friendship is an ongoing quest that involves taking risks and making an effort to be purposeful because ultimately it is the gift we give ourselves.

For Discussion and Reflection

1. Buzz relates the mixed responses he has had in taking even the first steps in building a more-than-casual friendship. What has been your experience? How have you dealt with rejection, and built on positive responses to move toward significant friendship?

2. Pat relates experiences of both building new relationships and sustaining those important long-term friendships. If you could give one piece of advice to another person or to yourself about developing deep soul friendships, what would it be?

3. What have you found is an important way of deepening existing friendships? How have you met new people?

Witness of Scripture: Friendship

The Bible records the full range of human relationships that we describe as friendship and is often keen to point out human failure. When the Psalmist writes, "There is no truth in their mouths; their hearts are destruction; their throats are open graves; they flatter with their tongues" (Ps. 5:9), he is describing human duplicity at its worst. Integrity of speech and fidelity of emotion are major building blocks in developing trust relationships. We long for what God longs for: human beings who "do not slander with their tongue, and do no evil to their friends, nor take up a reproach against their neighbors . . . who stand by their oath even to their hurt" (Ps. 15:3–4). Of course looking for such a friend is only part of the story. Equally important is to *be* such a friend, to practice integrity and honesty in our relationships.

In 1 Samuel 18:1–20:42, we read a description of the friendship of Jonathan and David. This passage reveals ways in which we can be better friends. In words attributed to Phillips Brooks[1] and others, Jonathon "forgot himself into immortality," through this extraordinary friendship. The last words between these two friends indicate that their bond was sealed by their love of God as well as their affection for one another: "The Lord shall be between me and you, and between my descendants and your descendants, forever" (1 Sam. 20:42). And after Jonathan died,

David acted on this covenant by bringing his friend's disabled son into his household (2 Sam. 9).

The covenantal nature of friendship is also illustrated in the intergenerational pairing of Ruth and Naomi. Often quoted at weddings, the words are spoken by the widowed daughter-in-law to her mother-in-law: "Where you go, I will go; where you lodge, I will lodge; your people shall be my people, and your God my God" (Ruth 1:16). Biblical friendship is about affection *and* long-term commitment, full of promise and deep devotion.

For Discussion and Reflection

1. What role does affection play in the relationship between Jonathan and David? (You may want to read again the opening verses of 1 Sam. 18.) When have you had a desire to cultivate a friendship with another person and it worked out well?

2 What role does commitment play in the relationship between Jonathan and David and between Ruth and Naomi? How important is commitment for you, even lifelong commitment, in friendships?

3. Given the high standard of friendship described in these two biblical examples, what does it mean for Jesus to call you "friend" (John 15:12–15)? What can you learn from him about friendship based upon the covenantal love of God?

Cultivating Friendship—A Spiritual Practice

As we enter into retirement, we may experience a loss of friendships related to employment, and so one key practice is cultivating new relationships around other interests. Medical science now knows that retirees with strong social networks are happier and healthier than those with few friends. Initiating new relationships and staying in touch with long-term friends are two important strategies for a vibrant life.

Christ-followers may long for more than golfing buddies and friendly neighbors, however. They may want to look for a spiritual friend, someone who will listen to their faith stories and their struggles and be willing to share the same in the spirit of mutuality. The notion of a spiritual friend dates back to 1150 CE when a monk by the name of Aelred wrote a series of essays on the topic. Aelred had been a member of the royal court, a nobleman; he knew about relationships built around power and pleasure. Tired of the court, he entered a monastery, not just any monastery but the strict order of the Cistercians (also known as the Trappists). Rising in the middle of the night to pray and subsisting on an austere diet, he was surprised to discover not only a deeper relationship with God but also a growing attentiveness and love for his monastic brothers. Aelred came to see the beauty of friendships that begin, continue, and find final confirmation in Christ.[2] Centuries later another Christian writer, C. S. Lewis, wrote a modern classic, *The Four Loves,* in which he states that friendship is the most spiritual love because it is the most free, and it is the one that can teach us the most.[3]

Is such friendship possible today? Is it something Christ followers should strive to develop? What if some became jealous of the intimacy shared? Christ himself knew these challenges, and yet he did not hold back from making deep spiritual friendships. You and I can do the same. If you long for a spiritual friend, pray for God to guide you to the right person. Listen as others share their faith and get a sense as to whether there's a kinship worth pursuing. Look for someone who can be a good listener as well as someone who can be vulnerable. Write down what you think you might want in a spiritual friendship and reflect on what you have written. Then when you are ready, talk to this person and see if he or she is being led in the same way.

One of us (Jerry) had a spiritual friendship for a number of years. Every month the two went hiking in nearby mountains. On the way up, one of the men talked about his faith and his struggles, while the other listened; on the way down, they reversed roles. They found this to be a very satisfactory way to "clear the air" as well as get some great exercise. Eventually a move out-of-state ended the arrangement, but both continue to value the time spent together.

5 Retiring *To* as Well as *From* Something

The phrase *it's about time* has been used as the title for about everything imaginable (e.g., a 2006 Jonas Brothers album, a 1966–67 sitcom on CBS, a committee promoting the legacy of the Black Panther Party, and a book on understanding Einstein's theory of relativity). This phrase is also descriptive of a life of fulfillment in retirement. Much of retirement is about time and how we spend it. As one man we interviewed correctly observed, "When I was working, the currency of my realm was money. Now that I am retired, it is time." Retirees who are spending this currency wisely have a sense that they are honoring God's call to significance in retirement.

One of the exciting realities that emerged in the interviews we conducted for our first book[1] was the wonderful and varied ways in which retirees use their time for the sake of others. In this chapter we first consider the experience of one retiree in moving to a life of contribution in retirement. We then explore the biblical insights on wise use of time and the promise of renewed strength as we wait on God for wisdom. Finally, we turn to the spiritual practice of discernment as the basis for selecting where and how to invest ourselves in this phase of life.

Experience of Retirees

Grant *(retired university professor)*

> I retired from a tenured professorship at a major university at age fifty-nine to pursue personal interests with greater freedom. It has now been eleven years since I made what seemed at the time a risky step into the unknown. In reality the events of the intervening years have taught my wife, Ruth, and me to listen better for God's direction and to perceive God's workings all around us in a more

consistent way. God has provided opportunities beyond our wildest dreams, enabling us to travel abroad to teach English in a developing country, and to develop lasting ties with students, colleagues, and church friends in that country.

Shortly after my retirement a former graduate student invited me to his country to give a series of lectures on teaching and testing for proficiency in English as a second language. My wife and I listened carefully for God's voice in this invitation and went. That visit led us to assume an intensely rewarding two-year faculty appointment in this country's newest national university. During this period we were privileged to not only have over one hundred undergraduate students in our classes but also to become involved in many of their lives. Those students have become like children to us; we have continued to be involved with them and with the university. We have assisted perhaps a dozen of these students to identify and pursue advanced study opportunities in the United States, and in fact three of them are living with us as they complete their studies at a nearby university. We have also continued to offer courses both on site at the university and through the technology of distance learning. Most importantly, several of these young people have come to experience God in their lives.

We also felt that we listened to God concerning our modest retirement savings. During an economic downturn after my retirement, it occurred to me that I should be more proactive with my own investments. This in turn led to the development of a mathematical model for stock selection and the writing and publication of a book concerning this experience. This has greatly expanded my world through reading, interactions, and even through a few invited lectures in this new field.

The point of these illustrations is that none of these exciting things could have happened if we had not been listening intently. I shudder to think what I would have missed if I had elected to stay in my secure job. I am deeply thankful for what has happened, both for my wife and me and in the lives of others, as we have sought to be attentive to God's provision and direction for us.

For Discussion and Reflection

1. Grant and his wife, Ruth, took a risky step by leaving a tenured faculty position for the unknown. How does one balance the need for security with this urge or calling to take risks? Notice that by taking this step, Grant and Ruth began listening to God more intently in their lives. When security becomes our focus, do we keep ourselves from hearing what God might be inviting us to do?

2. Grant and Ruth retired to an endeavor closely related to what they had done prior to retirement, namely teaching in higher education (though with many differences in context and compensation). What from your life experience, education, and career could help you discern a way to serve God and others in retirement? Is it possible that you are being called to something radically new?

3. Dream a bit. What would be your ideal post-retirement venture? What might you like to continue from your pre-retirement work? What do you want to let go of?

Witness of Scripture: Time and Timing

In the Greek language, there are two words for time: *chronos,* from which we get the word *chronology,* and *kairos,* which is more closely related to a sense of timing. Chronological time is the ticking of a clock and turning of the calendar. This notion of time rules and orders our everyday lives. If you are late, you miss the train, the bus, the opening act, or the appointment. Chronos is essential for efficient functioning in today's world. Kairos takes into account factors related to meaning, relationship, and context. Choosing when to ask someone to marry you, for example, may require a lot of thought about "the right (Kairos) moment."

In Scripture, both time and timing are important. In his letter to the church at Ephesus, Paul encourages his readers to make the most of the time (Eph. 5:15–16). The reality is that we are called to live each day faithfully and with thanksgiving for what God is doing in and through us.

The importance of timing is evident in Ecclesiastes 3:1–13, which tells us there is "a time for every purpose under heaven" (Eccl. 3:1, NKJV). "When is the best time to tell her?" we ask, when bad news needs to be said. "Timing is everything," comedians remind themselves. "Perhaps you have come to royal dignity for just such a time as this," Mordecai tells his cousin Esther (Esther 4:14). Jesus came in "the fullness of time" (Gal. 4:4); God's timing was perfect.

As we reflect on retiring to a life of greater responsiveness to God, both dimensions of time—chronos and kairos—are important. On a daily (chronological) basis, we want to use well what we have. We are invited to "count our days that we may gain a wise heart" (Ps. 90:12), which doesn't mean to rush around and fill every moment with mindless activity, but to live a healthy balance of activity and rest, leisure and service, and care of mind, body, and spirit.

We also seek God's timing as we ponder what God is calling us to do, which sometimes means waiting while discerning. Isaiah 40 -55 was written when Israel was still in captivity in Babylon, far from their cherished Promised Land. The prophet, referred to as Second Isaiah announces that a new world ruler, Cyrus the Great, will make it possible for them to return to Israel (cf. Isa. 44:28). But not quite yet. They must wait a little longer. Chapter 40 ends with the words "those who wait for the Lord shall renew their strength, they shall mount up with wings like eagles, they shall run and not be weary, they shall walk and not faint" (Isa. 40:31). We hate to hear the word *wait*. We're impatient and want to get on with things. Yet the Bible praises those who wait, for it is in waiting that we hear what God has to say to us. When we retire, we may still be in the getting-things-done mode. Still, if we are to hear God's call for us in retirement, we may need to learn to wait. In this waiting we receive both the wisdom and the strength to serve God and others.

For Discussion and Reflection

1. How do you feel about the possibility that there is a retirement vocation for which you have been prepared and to which you are being called? Do you have a sense of what it might be?

2. What steps of preparation might be important for you to discover or fulfill this unique calling?

3. Think about a past experience in which God's timing worked out better than your own planning. Note the ways that you saw God's timing—through a friend, as an answer to prayer, or as an inner sense of peace or consolation. Does this feel completely different than your work life, where you may have been praised for getting things done and being decisive rather than for waiting?

The Spiritual Practice of Discernment

Grant (see Experience of Retirees above) refers several times to how he and Ruth sought to "listen better for God's direction" in their lives. Such listening is the key to the spiritual practice of discernment. According to the dictionary to discern is to "see, know or detect."[2] In the Church over the centuries, discernment means seeking God's will, listening for God's call, and setting aside lesser claims on our lives. This is not easy to do because it means looking closely at ourselves. Are we willing to set aside our own agenda to hear what God has to say? Can we still the impatient voice inside of us that says *do something*? Do we really trust God to give us the guidance we need in our lives, perhaps even to take risks that rock the boat a bit?

Practically speaking, how do we practice discernment for the purpose of understanding God's calling for us in retirement? The first step is simply to pray, stating your intent to seek God's guidance for your retirement. You may want to draw upon Scripture for inspiration, such as Psalm 32:8: "I will instruct you and teach you the way you should go; I will counsel you with my eye upon you." The most important decisions take time, so a second step might be to write your thoughts in a journal on a daily basis. Ask yourself what brings you deep joy and a sense of satisfaction. Note also the times when you feel restless or unfulfilled. Ignatius of Loyola called these *consolations* and *desolations*, and they help us to pay attention to the inner GPS God has planted in our hearts.

Christians have long known that it is not good to make decisions alone. So the third step might be calling upon friends or family, asking them to pray for you as you wrestle with priorities and commitments and seek to respond to God's direction in your life. A prayer group at church or a Bible study group can be enormously beneficial in discernment, and can be a spiritual friend, as we discussed in chapter 4. Both authors of this resource have also participated in what the Quakers call a clearness committee. When Jack and his wife, Pat, were looking toward semi-retirement, they faced the decision of whether to accept a university teaching role or relocate closer to their grandchildren and invest more intentionally in their lives. They invited two wise and mature individuals to be their partners in discernment, and to serve as their clearness committee. These two individuals listened as Pat and Jack explained the options. They asked good questions. In the end Pat and Jack did not leave this session with an immediate sense of what they should do, but clarity did come as they reflected on the session, particularly the questions asked and their responses to these questions. (For more about clearness committees, see Parker Palmer's *A Hidden Wholeness.*[3])

Discernment is not magic; no matter how much we pray, ponder, and consult, we make mistakes. The benefit of practicing discernment is as much about confirming our true identity, hidden in Christ (Col. 3:3), as it is making sure-fire decisions that lead to success.

You may find it helpful to ask yourself the following questions as you reflect on this spiritual practice:

44

•Have I previously sought wisdom for a decision through a discernment process? Did I do this privately or in a group setting?

•Is there a matter right now about which I am seeking clarity? What is it? How might I proceed to seek God's wisdom through a discernment process?

6 Intellectual Growth and Creativity in Retirement

One of the must-sees in downtown Zurich is the Fraumünster Church. Since its construction in 853 CE, it has served as a convent and as a place of worship for Protestants, Roman Catholics, and Orthodox Christians. But its attraction today is five marvelous stained glass windows, designed by the artist Marc Chagall and installed in the late twentieth century. These windows are perhaps Chagall's best-known work. He designed them when he was eighty-three.

Chagall's remarkable late-in-life accomplishment reminds us of the importance of intellectual growth and creativity to a fulfilling retirement. Some retirees have described their involvement in university-based lifelong learning programs or distance learning opportunities. Others volunteer as teachers or mentors. Others are actively engaged in creative activities such as writing, painting, and photography. But regardless of the specifics, retirees described these pursuits to us enthusiastically and with a sense of self-discovery and delight.

In this chapter and the next, we examine intellectual growth and creativity separately from spiritual growth. In this chapter, focusing on intellectual growth, we consider the experience of two retirees in responding to the call to particular creative pursuits in retirement. Then, we examine Scripture passages in which such pursuits are mentioned. Finally, we explore the spiritual practice of service to others to illustrate the potential balance that a well-lived Christian life can offer.

Experience of Retirees

Tom *(retired professor of philosophy)*

Retirement was on the horizon. I knew it was coming. The stories people told didn't make it desirable: time on one's hands, no hope for meaningful activity beyond playing cards with friends (I do not like card games, except with my grandchildren), occasional volunteering, a loss of the definition of my life, a lot of history but no one to tell it to, deteriorating health, no one to hug. A crisis loomed; I could not go back to the past to recapture my old self, and did not see a new self in the future. I prayed for guidance. God did not answer by a voice in the night, a Damascus Road experience, or an insight during prayer. But God did answer.

Early in my career I knew God had something for me to say; what, I did not know. Now I felt a sense of calling to write the insights gained over many years of research after I left my teaching responsibilities. But how would this happen? If I left the university and the definition it provided, how would the call be answered?

Nevertheless, I set a retirement date; after forty-four years of life in higher education it was time (kairos) to fulfill the calling. As expected I felt the personal impact of losing all the external institutional structures that had defined my life. Facing my core, I asked, "Who am I apart from what I and others had fashioned for me?" I knew what I left behind; but I did not know what I faced now. Yet, amid the emptiness, the calling became clear.

As I molted, fearfully even in the presence of a quiet God, the vice-president for academic affairs and dean at the university approached me wondering if I would be interested in a five-year research position with only one responsibility: to write whatever I have to say. An office, all the resources of the university, and a generous stipend for books and travel would be provided. The university would leave me on my own to write whatever I cared to.

They had never provided this for anyone. The dean simply said he thought this would be a good idea. Then, I saw God's answer to my prayers. God provided the opportunity to obey my call.

Now, five years later, I feel that I have answered this late-in-life call. The two books that reflect what God has given me to say from a lifetime of teaching and learning have been published.

Wanda *(retired school counselor and university instructor)*

For thirty years I worked as a school counselor, administrator, and teacher, and followed that career with eleven years as an adjunct university instructor supervising graduate students in school counseling during their fieldwork. Then, in the late 1990s, I trained as a forensic interviewer of sexual abuse victims and did this work from time to time for several years.

In my late fifties, I decided to deepen my own spiritual practice, enrolling in a two-year spiritual direction program. That experience opened a door for me to work with others wishing to deepen their own journeys. At the same time, I began to once again pursue my lifelong love of photography, taking several classes, and plunging into the world of digital imaging.

In my early sixties, I stopped teaching and began focusing more intentionally on the spiritual life and doing deeper, more creative work with photography. While this was fulfilling at many levels, my soul still had the fidgets. Something was missing. I longed for some passion, a way to tap into and engage with the world that would bring healing.

The discovery of this missing passion began one winter morning. I was driving around randomly shooting photos. While usually a rich experience, on this particular morning I felt dejectedly like I was wasting time. Then I came to the country crossroads where one of my former students once lived. Suddenly, I remembered May 1973. I was finishing my first year as a school counselor when a fourteen-year-old honor roll student asked if I had time to talk. Sitting in my office, she poured out what would be one of the worst cases of sexual abuse that I would hear in my career. Forty years later, her words continued to haunt me. "He nailed the windows shut so we couldn't get out." I got chills remembering her story and countless others I had heard.

That night I had a dream. I am in the junior high where I began my career. Someone is saying, "Turn on the lights! Turn on the lights!" There are young women in orange jumpsuits standing in a line with their heads down. They look like they are imprisoned. Later in the dream, I meet a shy young woman who denies her talents as a photographer and I tell her emphatically that she is a photographer.

Through this series of synchronicities, I have this deep sense that I am to combine my work experiences, my photography, and the story lines of survivors to raise awareness in the community about sexual abuse. I follow this knowing and create a photographic story panel combining my student's words with my photo image of a dark window. When I finish, I know that I want to create a series of these story panels to release her story, the stories of others who have suffered and survived, and my own creative passion.

Over the next months, I talk to survivors. I work with a photo coach. I pursue an arts council grant. I secure community support. I find venues where this project will be used to raise awareness.

Just when I think this is done, more opportunities arise and I continue to immerse myself in the unfolding process.

I believe that the Spirit calls us to be part of the ongoing healing of the world. This project has been the way for me to offer my experience and creativity in the service of the greater good.

For Discussion and Reflection

1. Do you identify with any of the feelings that Tom had as he approached retirement? Do you find the prospect of leaving your full-time position unattractive, or if already retired, do you feel somewhat at sea without the institutional structure you were accustomed to in your work life?

2. What are some of the important differences in how Tom and Wanda came to realize their calling in retirement? Which resonates more with who you are? Why?

3. Do you have a feeling at this point that there is an unfilled task to which you are called in retirement?

Witness of Scripture: Intellectual Growth and Creativity

"You shall love the Lord your God with all your heart, and with all your soul, and with all your mind, and with all your strength" (Mark 12:30). Jesus is quoting Deuteronomy 6:5, affirming the wisdom of the Old Testament tradition. But wait a minute. The passage from Deuteronomy refers to heart, soul, and strength (or might), but there's no reference to one's mind. Did Jesus (or later New Testament editors) add something here? The mind as the location of one's intellectual ability may be implicit in the Hebrew trilogy, but the New Testament makes it explicit. Loving God with our mind is a holy thing to do.

The apostle Paul is a great example of one who loved God with his mind. Rising to prominence as a scholar within Judaism, his conversion brought a persuasive and articulate voice to the Christian faith. Some credit Paul as the primary agent in translating a parochial faith into world religion, capable of speaking to the needs of the Jews and non-Jews, urban Greeks, and Romans.[1] Other Old Testament and New Testament writers were equally gifted intellectually and the Christian message continued to attract the best minds of the ancient, medieval, and modern world (including St. Augustine, St. Thomas Aquinas, John Calvin, Hildegard of Bingen). No wonder John Wesley and others believed that faith is shaped by reason, as well as Scripture, tradition, and experience (the Quadrilateral).

Scripture also powerfully affirms the value of creativity. In Genesis 1, we hear that God created human beings imago Dei, in the image of God. Therefore, to be human is to create (though on a far lesser scale than the heavens and the earth). God's creativity is celebrated throughout Scripture (e.g. Ps. 148:5; Col. 1:16; Rev. 4:11) and so is human creativity. Hebrew poetry (for example, the Psalms) provides a creative response to the full range of experience, from devastating loss to greatest joy. The Bible also reveals a love of storytelling. Books like Jonah and Esther tell a story and in doing so convey theological truth that is easy to remember. And Jesus was a master storyteller, drawing uncommitted bystanders and casual listeners into the truth of God's love with powerful parables like the Prodigal Son and the Good Samaritan. Musical arts flourished under David with the Psalms, and the visual arts quickly gained importance in the Christian era. Human creativity truly is a way of honoring the Creator.

For Discussion and Reflection

1. What creative pursuit seems attractive to you at this point in your life? What might you do at this point to further explore and develop your creativity?

2. One component of intellectual activity in later life suggested in Scripture (e.g., Titus 2:3-4) is mentoring younger individuals. Are there mentoring roles for which you might be particularly well-suited in pre-retirement or retirement years or which you are engaged in now?

Creativity as Spiritual Practice

In her book *Creativity and Divine Surprise: Finding the Place of Your Resurrection,* Karla M. Kincannon invites readers to expand their notion of creativity. More than "art making," she suggests creativity is "a tool for navigating through everyday experiences to find the sacred in each God-given moment."[2]

In the second half of life, many gain new insights on life through creative expression. In the Experience of Retirees section, we saw how Wanda combined her creativity as an amateur photographer with her vocation as a sex abuse therapist to develop a resource for deep healing. While Wanda had been a photographer all her life, other retirees that we talked to cultivated artistic expression as they entered into retirement. Don, for example, had little time for painting while he was raising a family and pursuing a career in conflict mediation, but in his sixties he took a few classes and in retirement became an award-winning watercolorist. Don's religious background was highly conflicted, but through art he finds more serenity than he knew before. Buzz, whom we met in chapter 4, started writing in a journal every day when he retired, using a pattern described in Julia Cameron's book *The Artist's Way: A Spiritual Path to Higher Creativity.*[3] Others express their creativity through travel, gardening, committee work, or social events.

In recent years the theory of multiple intelligences developed by Harvard professor Howard Gardner has gained widespread acceptance.[4] In the 1980s Gardner realized that intelligence was often defined primarily or solely by linguistic and logical-mathematical competence. He expanded the notion of intelligence to include musical, spatial, bodily-kinesthetic, interpersonal, intrapersonal, and naturalistic ways of learning. Gardner's understanding of human intelligence has informed school curricula over the last several decades, but it also offers encouragement for adults who are looking for new ways to learn. In retirement these persons may feel challenged and energized as they develop skills in another type of intelligence.

Gardner's theory of multiple intelligences fits well with Kincannon's work on creativity. In her book Kincannon suggests exercises that use various tools for learning: watercolors, music, photography, silence, and journaling, no doubt to counter our culture's reliance on linguistic, interpersonal, and logical-mathematical competence. These exercises can help open us to the creative spark, but creativity, like prayer, is not the result of a simple how-to formula. Kincannon believes there is an encounter with the Divine Presence in every truly creative endeavor.[5] She also believes that creativity is part of our DNA, and like love it reflects the image of God within each of us. When we love and when we are creative, we are most at home in our identity as children of God.[6]

As persons called to be creative, we experience and respond to the world in ways that reflect the Divine Creator at work within us. Opening to alternative ways of knowing can facilitate this process and speak to a Spirit-hungry world. One of the authors of this book (Jerry) relied on interpersonal and linguistic skills in his work as a pastor. On a trip to Africa, however, he was amazed by the music and dancing in worship, and soon found himself moving down the aisle with the rest of the congregation. He reconnected with a bodily-kinesthetic way of praying as he danced to the beat of the drum. In that creative moment he understood the power of the Divine Encounter, even though he'll never win an award or dance on a Broadway

7 Spiritual Growth in Retirement

Several contemporary authors, including Gail Sheehy[1] and Abigail Trafford,[2] have written about spiritual development in later life from both sociological and spiritual perspectives. In his discussion of Protestant spirituality, Joseph D. Driskill notes that our spiritual orientation gradually changes in a positive way as we age. It becomes "less about correct behavior and more about ultimate trust in the God of the cosmos, who loves and blesses all creation and who sustains, transforms and leads us" even in the face of life's greatest difficulties.[3]

Post-retirement life has been a time of significant spiritual development for several of the men and women we interviewed and those we have interacted with in less structured settings.[4] Most note that a less hectic daily schedule provides time for the regular practice of prayer, reading, meditation, or other spiritual practices that contribute to a rich inner life. Though not explicitly stated, other factors may be at work as well, including a growing sense of our own mortality (the subject of chapter 10) and the realization that much of life is in fact beyond our own control.

In this chapter we shall focus on the experience of spiritual growth of one retiree, examples of late-in-life spiritual development in Scripture, and finally the spiritual practice of serving others in the development of our spiritual lives.

Experience of Retirees

Mary Jayne *(retired minister of Christian education)*

> Rising early was a necessity when I was a minister on the staff of an active congregation. Using some of those early morning hours for morning prayer and devotional reading has been my practice for years. With retirement I have learned that rising

early is actually my natural rhythm, and I'm delighted that without the necessity to leave for work I now have additional time for this practice. My husband and I agree to postpone conversation and other activities in the early morning, keeping silence for this time of personal devotions. Along with morning prayer, I'm enjoying reading devotional resources that have been untouched on my shelves as well as re-reading long-standing favorites.

Another practice that is somewhat easier with retirement is taking time for personal retreats. While I enjoy the sanctuary of our home, I find that getting away from familiar surroundings and tasks is an important part of my continuing spiritual growth and formation. A couple of days of solitude and silence feed my soul.

Accountability is an important aspect of my spiritual life. I am fortunate to meet regularly with a small group of women who are spiritual friends. Our time together includes a discussion of resources for spiritual growth, prayer, updates on personal and group ministry activities, and Communion. We encourage each other in spiritual practices. We all agree that it is important to be in community as part of our spiritual journey and ministry.

Being connected with a larger community of faith is also important. Worship and service with my local congregation has always been a significant part of my life. As long as I am able, I want to continue to be an active participant in teaching and learning, corporate worship, and ministry with fellow believers.

When asked, "How are you enjoying retirement," many people will answer, "I'm busier than ever." With the freedom from the structure of work, we are faced with numerous opportunities to volunteer at church and in the community. It is easy to become like Martha in Luke's Gospel—"distracted by many things"—and neglect Mary's choice of "the better part"—the opportunity to sit and listen to the Lord. I want to be intentional in these latter years of my life—active in ministry and service, but using the gift of time to be still and enjoy God's loving presence.

For Discussion and Reflection

1. Mary Jayne highlights the importance of daily devotions to her, both when working and now in retirement. What challenges have you experienced in seeking to incorporate such a practice during your work life? What has been, or do you anticipate will be, different in retirement?

2. More generally, do you find that being still and enjoying God's presence comes naturally to you, or is your orientation more toward action? Are there practical aids that you find helpful in focusing on God's presence in a meaningful way?

Witness of Scripture: Spiritual Growth in Later Life

The Bible offers us numerous examples of spiritual development in the later stages of life. Abraham is but one example. Very late in life he was called upon by God to leave the familiarity of his homeland and his extended family for a new place and a new life, one that would make him the father of a great nation. Our own personal history may provide additional examples. We may be fortunate to know an older man or woman whose spiritual maturity and example have contributed to our own spiritual journey.

The author of Hebrews reminds us of the lives of some of these giants of faith in Hebrews 11. Chapter 12 highlights key characteristics of these individuals' faith journeys, so that we may be encouraged and challenged in our own faith journeys. He writes,

Therefore, since we are surrounded by so great a cloud of witnesses, let us also lay aside every weight and the sin that clings so closely, and let us run with perseverance the race that is set before us, looking to Jesus, the pioneer and perfecter of our faith . . . Consider him who endured such hostility against himself from sinners, so that you may not grow weary or lose heart. (Heb. 12:1–3)

The admonition to lay aside unnecessary weights is relevant at any age. In our later years such unnecessary weights may come in the form of past grievances and resentments that resurface as we reflect on the past. These need to be worked through and released in order to find inner peace and freedom. Persevering in spiritual practices can help the older person gain a more gracious perspective. To draw on the athletic metaphor of the author of Hebrews, endurance is not a challenge early in the race, when we are fresh and the event is still in its early stages. Instead, endurance becomes the key issue as the race goes on. We get tired, and the finish line is not yet in view. It is in these later stages of the race of life that we may be particularly tempted to slack off or get discouraged.

For Discussion and Reflection

1. Who has been a particularly influential member of the cloud of witnesses in your life, living his or her later years in a way that has encouraged you? What is it about his or her character that stands out to you?

2. At this stage of your pre-retirement or retirement life is there a circumstance or situation that tests your endurance or causes you to call into question your own ability to endure for the long term? What about this are you finding particularly difficult?

The Spiritual Practice of Service to Others

A school administrator, exhausted from budget battles and parent-teacher conflicts, spent several hours preparing sandwiches for the local homeless shelter. She was surprised that the work brought a sense of renewal and purpose to her life. A corporate executive got in touch with his God-given sense of compassion while volunteering at an alcoholic treatment facility. A burned-out pastor searching for a better prayer life found himself praying with renewed passion while sheltering a group of homeless and unemployed men for the night.

Each of these is an example of the spiritual value of serving others, yet such spiritual growth was a secondary byproduct. As Christ-followers, these volunteers sought to care for the least, the last, and the lost, providing food, comfort, and care for those in need. Something else happened-the volunteers began to sense that Christ Himself was present in the needy they sought to serve (Matt. 25:31–46).

In this book we have emphasized spiritual practices focused on our growth as Christians during transition into retirement. These include such practices as witness, prayer, and companionship, which we may not have fully developed earlier in life. To balance this list, we include a reminder of the great value of giving oneself to others through service. Such "works of mercy," as Wesley called them, are also means of grace.

For many retirees, having time to serve others is one of the great gifts of this stage of life. After retiring as teachers, Dan and Joyce spent sixteen years living in an RV and going from mission project to building project in various states as volunteers in NOMADS.[5] Another retiree, Ken was a local church pastor for forty years. Then, in his "retirement," he took on the job of State Coordinator for the Michigan chapter of Habitat for Humanity. After years of being on the receiving end of Christian nurture from their church, Wes and Helen decided to dedicate their retirement years to giving to others. They had served on committees before but now they wanted to be involved in direct service. They went through extensive training in Stephen Ministry and learned the art of caregiving, helping many through life's most difficult transitions.

8 Called to Caregiving

As our parents age, we become aware that we may need to be their caregivers at some point. We may also be called upon for other caregiving responsibilities. Among the retirees we have interviewed were those caring for spouses, siblings, adult children, and grandchildren. Some cases were due to illness or accident and others the result of adult children unable to carry out parental responsibilities.[1]

In this chapter we will consider the experience of one retiree who was unexpectedly called to be a caregiver early in retirement. Then we will refer to Scripture with its witness to the compassionate nature of God, and how we are called to emulate it. And finally, we consider the spiritual practice of corporate worship as a key to the health of the caregiver.

Experience of Retirees

Nancy *(retired professor and head of an academic department)*

> On a spring day several years ago I walked into the president's office to return my contract for the coming year. He seemed surprised that I was returning the contract for only one more semester. The workload of a department chair at a small liberal arts college includes preparing reports for national accreditation and other reports for state agencies, along with creating syllabi, teaching classes, grading papers, and serving on various committees, and all this was taking a toll on my eyes. By the end of the year I would be eligible for Social Security and Medicare and the idea of some relaxation and travel was appealing.
>
> My request turned out to be a "God

thing." There was no way that I could anticipate what that fall semester would bring. In early fall my daughter was injured in an auto accident, when two other cars hit her car while she was waiting for a stoplight to change. The head injury caused some permanent damage, especially to short-term memory. In addition, my sister was teaching middle school, fighting ovarian cancer, and taking care of a legally blind husband with other disabilities. By the end of the fall semester I was making a three-point circuit from my apartment to my daughter's house an hour away, then three hours north to my sister's, and finally back to my place to pay bills, get clean clothes, say hello to friends, and then start my rounds again. I had been called into caregiving for two women who are very dear to me.

My sister passed two years after I retired and after she had undergone a second surgery and chemotherapy. She was thankful she got to meet her newborn first grandchild a few months before her death. She also got to hold him at Christmas and once in the spring. My sister was ten years younger than I and we had planned on spending our retirement years together, because her husband's disabilities suggested she would be a widow at some point. Losing her was not a part of my retirement plan. Grief can still overcome me at times.

My daughter is a brilliant attorney who realized after her accident that she needed to find an alternate career and lifestyle. We found a place in the country where she tends a large organic garden and does legal work that does not require the conflict of courtroom arguments. I became the housekeeper and financial manager.

The organized church is a blessing when you move often. In the nearby small town I was welcomed and soon was serving on committees. I became chair of the Christian Education and Nurture Committee, led Disciple Bible Studies, organized an intergenerational Vacation Bible School, and took the opportunity to attend the two-year Academy for Spiritual Formation, which offered a rich time of spiritual growth along with fifty other spiritual companions. Since then I have also completed two years of the three-year program our conference sponsors for Parish Christian Educators.

No, I did not plan to feed chickens and gather eggs in my retirement. Nor did I expect to be tending an orchard of about thirty peach and plum trees. I've learned how to make jelly and preserves as well as to freeze fruits and vegetables. I can report that watering the fruit trees and grape and berry vines does provide a wonderful time for prayer. My vision of retirement was not at all accurate, but it has become much richer than I expected. Praise God.

For Discussion and Reflection

1. Have you had the responsibility of caring for a loved one on a temporary basis at some point in your adult life? What did you take away from this experience?

2. Among the caregiving responsibilities that may come in later life (parent, spouse, adult child, grandchild, other relative), which do you think you might find most difficult and why?

3. As you read about these experiences of caregiving, as well as your own, what do you see as some key elements of coming to view this responsibility as a calling?

Witness of Scripture: Compassionate Caregiving

God's compassion is celebrated throughout the Scriptures, Old and New Testament. That compassion is seen, for example, in the divine covenant with us (see 2 Kings 13:23). God's care for us serves as the model for how we are to care for and have empathy for others, including strangers. "Love [the stranger] as yourself, for you were [strangers] in the land of Egypt . . . " (Lev. 19:34). Those who are most vulnerable, the widow, the orphan, and the stranger, command God's care and deserve society's protection (e.g. Ps. 146:9, Jer. 7:6, 22:3). Holiness and compassion form the basis for righteousness in the Old Testament.

God's passionate regard for others is even more evident in the New Testament. Faithful, compassionate love shines through Christ in numerous healing stories and especially in the care he extended to the Jairus' daughter (Mark 5:21–43) and the centurion's slave (Luke 7:1–10). Both Jairus (a leader of the synagogue) and the centurion (a Roman soldier) represent potential enemies of Jesus, yet Jesus' compassion extends to enemies, not just his family and friends.

Jesus looked for compassion in others. In a dramatic story in Mark 2:1–12, four friends lower a paralyzed man through a roof, to place him before Jesus. Seeing the risky caregiving of the friends, Jesus heals the man, not because of *his* faith but because of *their* faith (vs. 5). Caregiving is not just something that Jesus did; it is something all of us are called to do. We are to "bear one another's burdens, and so fulfil the law of Christ" (Gal. 6:2, RSV).

Compassionate caregiving is more than a passing impulse. It is built on the covenantal love of God for us that serves as the basis of our relationship with family and friends. In chapter 4, "Retirement and Friendship," we mentioned one of the best-known accounts of caregiving in the Bible—the story of Ruth and Naomi. The care of a mother-in-law and daughter-in-law for one another illustrates what the Hebrew Bible called "steadfast love" (*hesed*). This is covenantal love. It is bound by oath and loyalty transcending whims and feelings. It is a deeply vowed love, one that goes beyond the moment. It is based on everything a person has to give and more.

Such love has its own reward. It feeds the one who gives because it affirms the truth of who we are. God did not make us for ourselves alone, but for others as well. The supreme example is

Jesus Christ. In giving up his life, he showed what it truly means to live. The force and power of this love still empowers those called to the ministry of caregiving today.

For Discussion and Reflection

1. In your opinion, what makes for healthy caregiving and receiving relationships? In what ways do you see God's *hesed* love in the story of Ruth and Naomi? What lessons might be applicable to a modern-day circumstance?

2. Retirees of today are often called on to care for children and younger adults. As you reflect on the examples of care and guidance given by Eli for Samuel (1 Sam. 1–3) and Mordecai for Esther (Esther 4), what parallels or lessons are applicable to relationships you have now with younger people in your life (grandchildren, nieces and nephews, neighbors, etc.)?

The Value of Spiritual Community

Caregiving has multiple challenges. It is common to hear from caregivers stories of loneliness, isolation, and lack of rest.[2] These can lead to exhaustion and illness so that the caregiver also needs care. Spiritual practices that retain a connection with the larger body of believers are essential for those giving care. Marjorie J. Thompson points out that our spiritual practices need to be supported, broadened, clarified, and sometimes corrected through corporate experience.[3] When the stress of caregiving is particularly acute, slipping in and out of worship may be about the most that the caregiver can handle. On other occasions, more interaction with others in a Sunday morning class or small group might be helpful. Regular Sunday morning worship attendance is one way to build in a break for oneself. A Sunday school class, a small group, or a spiritual friendship can help to relieve the isolation that may occur. Devotional resources such as *Not Alone: Encouragement for Caregivers*[4] or *The Upper Room* magazine[5] may bring the voices of other caregivers close. Occasionally, a longer respite—perhaps a quiet retreat—may be needed. In whatever form, the discipline of regular contact with the body of believers is perhaps the most important practice for caregivers. The times of loneliness and isolation in giving care may be unavoidable, but participation in corporate worship and the fellowship of a small group provides continued encouragement to see caregiving as a calling and a ministry.

9 Meeting Declines in Physical Capabilities

We are a society that values physical prowess. The emphasis we place on remaining physically fit through regular exercise and healthy diet is but one indication of this reality. There is ample evidence that such measures are beneficial to our health at every age. And yet even the most physically fit among us will experience declines in physical capabilities with age.

Most of the retirees that we interviewed for our first book were in quite good health when they retired (although some had significant health challenges). Nevertheless, even those who were healthy expressed the realization that their physical capabilities had declined to some extent. For some, the changes since retirement had been relatively minor, such as reduced energy levels. Others had witnessed more significant physical changes and challenges in these years (e.g., significantly reduced mobility). The key question articulated by those who were already experiencing physical challenges was how can I live with grace and thanksgiving while these changes occur?[1]

In this chapter we consider the perspectives of a man living with physical limitations and of a retired physician. Then we shall seek to discover the scriptural perspective on the loss of the physical capabilities we once had. And finally, we identify one personal practice that may be particularly important to our continuing to live for the sake of others in this phase of life.

Experience of Retirees

Jim *(retired pastor of a major Protestant denomination)*

> I had retired at sixty-five and was still as good as ever at seventy, doing serious race walking and carrying out projects around the house as I always had. I saw no reason I couldn't carry on the

same level of activity indefinitely.

But now I've passed my seventy-fifth birthday, and all that has begun to change. Joints hurt. Floaters are showing up in my field of vision. My favorite three-mile walk takes longer. I have less and less stamina. Worst of all, no matter how hard I try my performance simply refuses to improve. I have become an old man.

There was never any reason to imagine that things would be otherwise, of course. A quick review of my life revealed a whole series of such changes, after all—the reshaping of skeleton and muscles that attended the passage from childhood to adolescence, the improvement in small motor control that went with the move into young adulthood, the rearrangement of fat and muscle that marked my entry into middle adulthood. It was all part of growing up.

The hardest thing about the transition to old age, perhaps, has been the need for help with tasks that a short time ago I could have done myself. At the store where we buy seed for the wild birds, I always would load the forty pound bags into the car myself. No more. Now one of the young men shows up from nowhere, smiles, and says, "Here, let me get that." And the worst of it is that I'm glad for the help.

Then there's the annual banquet our daughter and son-in-law serve to family and friends. I have always been one of the kitchen crew, making coffee and washing pots and pans. It's strenuous work, and I've always enjoyed taking my part. Only now I no longer have the stamina for it. Now my role is to meet guests and converse with them. That's pleasant enough, but it's not helpful in the way I'd like to be helpful.

Hence the issue: how do you live life in a meaningful way when you can no longer do all the things you've always done? Old age imposes limits on us, and we have to learn how to live within those limits.

The key to living fully during our later years is the same as during our earlier years. It depends on learning that life must be lived according to a vocation. It's not merely a matter of finding what we enjoy or what might win the highest rewards (money, respect, or whatever). Rather, it's discovering what we are called to do. The new limits imposed by advancing age bring paradoxically a new freedom. What determines our choice is not money, hope for advancement, or prestige. Rather, it is the great question, what is it we were born to do? Coming to the answer may require meditation, introspection, or perhaps counseling, but the answer is there, waiting to be found.

Leslie *(retired physician)*

I believe many of us view the aging process as starting at some point around age sixty-five, but physiologically we hit our peak in our late teens and early twenties and it's downhill from there. As a post sixty-five-year-old I like to think that spiritual growth or maturing in faith need never go downhill, that life experiences are capable of molding us spiritually if we are able to be open to that possibility.

In my forty-plus years of medical practice as a primary care physician in general internal medicine and most recently as a hospice physician, I have not only experienced my own aging process and limitations, but have been privileged to be a companion in small and major ways for brief periods

67

and for the majority of a lifetime to many who have called me their doctor. I have observed, shared, attempted to guide, rejoiced with, and sorrowed with those in transitions through many stages of life, health, and circumstances. I have seen the full spectrum of how we humans deal with the realities of the aging process, emotionally and spiritually.

If following a list of dos and don'ts in regard to aging could guarantee a vital and active old age, many people would have that list taped to their bathroom mirror or memorized. Even though following a healthy lifestyle can have a huge impact on our later life, the gradual effects of aging continue, and acute and devastating illnesses still occur.

As I have recognized some of the sure indications of increasing age in myself, I think back over the years of practice and how variable have been the responses to aging in my patients. For example, there are the angry deniers—those who cannot accept that a painful ankle while running can happen to them. They expect and demand complete resolution of symptoms (and make sure it's in time to run a marathon in a week). Then there are the passive accepters who assume that all symptoms are due to normal aging and often fail to seek medical attention and are at risk of missing more serious, potentially correctable, or treatable conditions. The third group is the realistic accepters. These persons accept that some physical and mental decline is inevitable and try to become and stay informed about what to expect in the normal course of aging versus those signs or symptoms that may be red flags of more serious problems. A fourth group might be the worried well—those who are certain that every symptom represents life-threatening disease.

I realize that we humans are more varied and complex than to fit into any neat category and in reality we probably all at one time or another may be in one or several of the above categories. But in all likelihood, we may see ourselves gravitate toward one of these styles.

I have often speculated about the relationship between our spirituality and our perspective on aging and decline. Certainly it seems that many strive mightily with God in wondering *why me?* Or *what did I do to deserve this?* Others may accept their problems by feeling that this is some punishment for known or unknown affronts to God and do not even pursue the possibility of relief or cure. I have seen many over the years who seem to maintain a beautiful equanimity in the face of much more severe problems than normal aging limitations. While they don't deny themselves any and all efforts at cure or alleviation of symptoms, they maintain a peace, a sense of humor, and a deep compassion and thoughtfulness of others. For them I believe the loving kindness of God is a real presence. Rather than question the why or challenge their Deity, they have a real and profound knowledge of the Divine Presence loving them and even suffering with them.

Could it be that our gradual aging is God's way of helping us to begin to realize and then come to terms with our own mortality? The whole human race has this project in common and we all must at one time or another face the ultimate reality of our own demise. Ernest Becker wrote an extremely important book—*The Denial of Death*—in the 1970s.[2] He posits in this book that underlying most if not all of our many attachments, addictions, and self-defeating actions and activities lies a universal deep denial of our own mortality. He doesn't claim any specific spiritual dimension to his philosophy, but it seems to me that there must be a connection between our sense of and relationship with the Divine and our ability to live and die peacefully and gracefully.

For Discussion and Reflection

1. Jim notes the things that are hard for him about declining physical capabilities, but at the same time affirms a sense of calling for this phase of life. How might you live out your calling when you reach Jim's phase of life?

2. Leslie highlights the various ways that his aging patients react to their changing physical abilities (angry deniers, passive accepters, realistic accepters, worried well). Which group do you see yourself most like in temperament and orientation?

Witness of Scripture: Reduced Physical Capabilities

As in so many other areas of life, the Scripture gives a different perspective on limited physical capabilities than the messages we receive from our culture. Consider, for example, the events surrounding Mary and Joseph taking Jesus to the temple a few days after his birth (Luke 2:22–38). There they encounter two remarkable people, Simeon and Anna. Anna is eighty-four years old, a widow of many years, and Simeon is an old man. Yet while they are old physically, with the attendant reduction in physical capabilities, they are totally alert spiritually. Both of them sense that God has entered the temple with this family and something profound is about to happen. Like any other day, the temple was populated that day with large numbers of priests and worshipers. But of all of these, only Simeon and Anna saw the holiness in this family.

And Simeon and Anna are by no means the only individuals in Scripture with physical limitations who are used in unique ways by God. The apostle Paul writes of a "thorn in the flesh" that he lives with (2 Cor. 12:7–10). He does not say what this affliction was, though many have speculated that it was poor eyesight. Regardless of its nature, we know that Paul asked God to remove it from him.

70

But God's response was that "my grace is sufficient for you, for my power is made perfect in weakness" (2 Cor. 12:9, RSV).

For Discussion and Reflection

1. Declining physical capabilities are a natural part of aging, but the same is not necessarily true of our spiritual capacities. What do you see in the lives of Simeon and Anna that contributed to spiritual growth with age, even as their physical capabilities declined?

2. Paul's physical limitation was not associated with age. Nevertheless, how does an unwanted physical limitation seem to be used of God to continue to form this man in God's image?

The Practices of Intercessory Prayer and Encouragement

The personal reflection by Jim is perceptive in focusing on what we are called to do in this phase of life. Some individuals we know have been called to ministries of intercessory prayer. For example, one of us (Jack) at one time had the privilege of being among the quarter million or so college and graduate students in the Boston area. Many among the Christian student population there were aware of the ministry of an elderly woman, known as Aunt Tib, who suffered from a condition that had limited her physical mobility from young adulthood. And yet, she was connected to numerous college students and ministries in a vibrant way. She both hosted individual students in her apartment as her strength permitted, and regularly prayed for a large number of Christian students by name. The vitality of the Christian student ministry in Boston seemed directly tied to the prayer ministry of this one faithful woman. Her faithfulness had an impact that was most likely beyond that of others who served in more visible ways.

Closely related to and perhaps growing out of this practice is the capacity for encouragement. We were reminded of the potential for ministry to others in this way by the example of Huston Smith, who for many years was a well-known professor of philosophy and religion. When he was ninety-one and living in an assisted living

71

facility, he wrote in the last part of his autobiography, *Tales of Wonder*, "People go to nursing homes, I have heard it said, to die. I came to this assisted living residence, it seems, to cheer people up. Every morning I mentally take a census of every resident here. And as each person appears in my imagination, I ask myself and God, 'how can I improve his or her day?'"[3] What a wonderful example in this phase of life of the spiritual practice of encouragement commended by the apostle Paul with the words, "Encourage one another and build one another up" (1 Thess. 5:11, RSV).

10 We Won't Live Forever

At one time or another, each of us has had an encounter or experience that changed everything—our future, our outlook, and our values. For some this may have been our first meeting with the person who would become our spouse. For others, it may have been the birth of a child. Or, it may have been a career-related event, such as a promotion, recognition, or even retirement. For still others, it has been an unpleasant experience such as an illness, accident, or untimely death of a loved one.

As we read the New Testament and enter into the experiences of the men and women who knew Jesus, we realize that the single event that changed everything for them was encountering the Risen Christ. Beginning with this event we begin to see radical changes in their understanding of who Jesus was, who they were, and how they would spend the remainder of their lives. And, particularly pertinent to the topic of this chapter, a fundamental change in how they understood death and life after death.

Coming to grips with our own mortality is one of the specific challenges that retired men and women identified for us in the interviews conducted for our first book.[1] They realize that it is no longer adequate to think, as we so commonly do in our society, that death is a distant reality. For some, this realization grew out of involvement with a friend or loved one in the final stages of life; for others it arose through their own illness or injury. In this chapter we consider the experience of one retiree as he dealt with his father's dying. Then, we consider one account from the Gospel of Luke and one from the writings of Paul to understand what the New Testament says about death, life beyond, and implications for the present. And finally, we turn to one personal practice that has the potential to help each of us to think about our own mortality in a way consistent with these truths.

Experience of Retirees

Bruce *(retired pastor and seminary professor)*

In the year between my father's heart attack and his death, the two of us had many opportunities for long talks. We spoke about all sorts of things, including his thoughts and feelings about death. While in the hospital my father had undergone a near-death experience. He recalled it vividly and remembered entering a long tunnel with a brilliant light at the end. As he walked toward the light my father could see a group of people approaching him and among them he was able to recognize his mother and father. He was filled with awe and wonder and joy as he anticipated a glad reunion with those he loved. In the midst of this event he recalls making a decision to turn around and return to my mother and me.

When he recovered consciousness my father knew that his life had been radically changed by this experience. He was, he said, no longer fearful of death or afraid to die. His days from that point onward were without anxiety and he was filled with a new and lasting sense of peace. Each day became a gift, a gift of freedom instead of a time to be grasped as if it were his last.

Our conversations led to the planning of his funeral service. He wanted to have this service witness to his personal discovery of the power of the Easter experience at the heart of the Gospel and the faith of the Church. That would have been all but impossible given the way funerals took place in the town from which my parents came. Mourners gathered in the funeral home and not the church. The service consisted of readings and prayers—prayers for everyone except the one who died. It was as if he were gone and no longer existed. The eulogies were designed to praise the accomplishments of the one who died and seldom spoke about God's grace, the Resurrection, or the hope for eternal life, except in sentimental ways. My father wanted, for the sake of his family and friends, to break away from all of that and so he asked me to be the major celebrant and to take responsibility for conducting his funeral service. Whether he understood it or not, this was the most difficult thing that my father ever asked me to do. It was also, as it turned out, one of the greatest gifts that he ever gave me.

The service itself was a celebration of Easter. It included powerful witnesses from Scripture, preaching on the promises of the gospel, and a celebration of the Eucharist, the Lord's Supper. At my father's insistence, the reflections on his life pointed not to his successes but to the trials and difficulties in which he had experienced the grace and presence of God. But what remains strongest in my memory came at the beginning of the service when I welcomed everyone and told them that the newspaper accounts were wrong indicating the date of his death, as my father asked me to do. His death had not taken place on February 6, 1978, but on May 23, 1912, the day of his baptism. From that day onward, whether conscious of it or not, my father understood that he had been given a new gift of life in Christ from whom not even death itself could separate him. Christ is risen. He is risen indeed.

It is now many years later. I am older than my father was at the time of his death. I live now in retirement and have more time to reflect. A recent illness and surgery are reminders of my own mortality. Thanks in part to my father, I do not find thinking about death, including my own, as a morbid or an anxious experience, but a reminder that each day is a gift to be given away freely to others with as much imagination, creativity, and love as grace allows. Better still, this is the secret source of that joy that overcomes the world.

For Discussion and Reflection

1. Has there been an event in your life in the last few years that has made you more aware of your own mortality, and if so was the effect transient or lasting?

2. For you, how does your spirituality influence your feelings about your mortality? Is this at a heart-level, or is it more intellectual?

Witness of Scripture: Death and Resurrection

Luke 24 allows us to see the initial realization of Jesus' resurrection through the eyes of some of his closest followers. The women who went to his tomb to anoint his body with burial spices found no body to anoint, but instead an empty tomb and a declaration by angels that Jesus had been raised from the dead. That same day, two men who had followed Jesus were walking from Jerusalem to Emmaus. A stranger joined them and inquired what they were talking about. They expressed sadness as they described Jesus' death. The stranger proceeded to explain how these events were foretold in the Old Testament Scriptures. When he joins them for supper, they recognize him as the risen Jesus. Still later in the day Jesus appears to some of his followers who are gathered together in Jerusalem.

In each of these encounters with the Risen Christ, the disciples respond first with puzzlement and fear. No one anticipated his overwhelming Presence after his brutal death. These emotions were followed by deep joy, however, and a sure confidence in God's love triumphant over death that continues to guide the Church today.

How shall we understand this story today? As New Testament scholar N. T. Wright points out in his excellent book on the topic of death, resurrection, and implications for the present, we live in a world of "now but not yet."[2] The New Testament affirms that life beyond life is real, that we will live as spiritual bodies (1 Cor. 15), and that all creation anticipates a new heaven and new earth (Rev. 21). In the present we experience only a part of this reality, along with a freedom from anxiety about death. This freedom opens entirely new possibilities to serve others in Christ's name and power. We no longer live for ourselves, but focus instead on following Jesus. In the words of Paul, we are convinced that "neither death, nor life, nor angels, nor rulers, nor things present, nor things to come . . . will be able to separate us from the love of God in Christ Jesus our Lord" (Rom. 8:38–39).

For Discussion and Reflection

1. What is one experience that changed everything for you, as did the Resurrection of Jesus for the early disciples? To what extent were you conscious of how much had changed at the time, or did you come to appreciate the implications of the experience or encounter only later?

2. The disciples, like us, lived in a time when there were all kinds of answers to the question of what lies beyond the grave. How do you think the experience of Jesus' resurrection impacted the manner in which they answered this question for themselves?

3. Over the years the early church had a growing realization that we are incapable of fully understanding what life beyond the grave will be like. It is a "wonder beyond words," one that for the present we can only "see through a glass darkly" in Paul's words at the end of I Cor. 13. How do you see this "wonder beyond words" in such passages as 1 John 3:1–3 and Revelation 21:10–21?

4. Jesus' resurrection underscored to his closest followers his promise to them that he would send a helper, "the Spirit of truth that . . . abides with you, and . . . will be in you" (John 14:16–17). How did this promise impact them, and how does it impact us?

The Practice of Thanksgiving in all Things

A recently published collection of writings and lectures by Henri Nouwen highlights the importance of moving from denying to befriending death before our own death is imminent.[3] Critical to making this step in Nouwen's view is regaining our own deep sense that we are God's beloved. This may happen as a result of being injured or ill ourselves, going through this experience with others, or some seemingly unrelated experience that causes us to realize anew and more deeply the extent of God's love and care for us.

Knowing that we will die, as God's beloved we know even more fully that death will not separate us from the love of Christ. In that knowledge we respond as Paul does: "Rejoice always, pray without ceasing, give thanks in all circumstances; for this is the will of God in Christ Jesus for you" (1 Thess. 5:16–18), In other words, the life of thanksgiving in all things is at the heart of a rich life in Christ.

Psalm 92 likewise commends a life of praise and suggests that it is the secret of liveliness: praise for the God of *hesed* (steadfast love), praise in the morning and praise at night (vs. 2). The regular rhythm of praise at morning and at night is a habitual pattern, a way to bring one's life regularly before God. As we age, the pattern of giving thanks may be even more important to maintain, since it is sometimes easy to become depressed or cynical. And when we face death, giving thanks to God for the life we have been given connects us with the whole of one's life, transcending the final hour. On his deathbed, John Wesley is reported to have whispered the words to the hymn, "I'll praise my Maker while I've breath; / and when my voice is lost in death, / praise shall employ my nobler powers."[4]

Verses 5 through 11 of Psalm 92 reflect a different tone. Enemies and evil have been overcome; stupidity has been defeated. The author appears to be celebrating some specific triumph, though we don't know the details. Perhaps it was the enemy we call death that was defeated by God's love.

Do we take the time to rejoice when things go well? Can we give thanks even when things do not go so well? If this is hard for us, we can grow in our faith as we age, just like the palm tree and the cedar celebrated in verse 14 of the Psalm. We too can stay "green and full of sap" as we live in God's love.

11 Retirement and Personal Identity

Our self-concept and feeling of worth derive from the roles, responsibilities, and relationships we have through much of our adult life. But as we approach and enter into retirement, many of these underpinnings change. We may go from the structure of a profession or job to relatively unstructured days. Our responsibilities in the home, and to our spouse if married, may shift significantly (e.g., more day-to-day responsibilities in the home). Collegial work relationships may end, and relocation (ours or friends) can further disrupt our network of friends. The sense that everything has changed may be even more acute if we lose a spouse or experience major changes in our health.

These practical realities require us to answer the most fundamental of questions. Who am I now that I am retired? And how can I continue to have a sense of self-worth and purpose? Such questions were central to many of the conversations we have had with retired men and women. In this chapter we consider the words of one retiree who expressed these fundamental questions. Then we look at sections of Scripture in which individuals are forced to answer similar questions in the midst of change and uncertainty. Lastly, we consider a practice that may contribute to our sense of purpose and well-being.

Experience of Retirees

Richard Morgan, a retired Presbyterian pastor, recalls a terrifying moment early in retirement. Here in its entirety is a meditation he wrote in his book *I Never Found that Rocking Chair: God's Call at Retirement.*[1]

> I had to introduce myself at a meeting
> as a retired person. It petrified me. Others
> there told where they worked or described

80

their most recent trip or work-related project. My own description—"retired"—sounded so ominous, so empty. Two words seemed to fit, "has been." I managed to blurt out, "I am retired, but still active," as if I needed to apologize for no longer being in the full-time work force. I was a victim of the retirement disease known as "used-to-beism."

Saul, the first king of Israel, suffered the same disease. At first his star had shone brightly: "There is none like him among all the people" (1 Sam.10:24, RSV). He reached the pinnacle when he smashed the Ammonites, sent the Philistines scurrying back to their land, and vanquished Israel's enemies. But he could not win the inner battle and began to be threatened by the loss of his throne. David becomes his therapist, but also his rival. Soon, David, with his smashing victories and charismatic personality, eclipses Saul; and Saul is rejected as king.

Saul's decline is vividly seen in scenes from the wilderness of Ziph, where David spares his life. "Behold, I have played the fool, and have erred exceedingly," he says (1 Sam. 26:21, RSV). Saul is a tragic hero, more to be understood than condemned, one who errs but whose story points the way to wholeness.

Nothing creates more depression in retirement years than the feeling of uselessness. Nothing hurts more than feeling you are "out of mind like one who is dead" [Ps. 31:12, RSV]. No one likes to think of themselves as a person who *used-to-be* valued, productive, and of worth.

Life is not to be seen as a peak, with an upward and downward side, as if retirement means automatic consignment to the world of has-beens. Life has peaks and valleys at any age. And I cannot but believe that there is more for us to do in the midst of life beside simply watch it from the balcony.

Retirement is an opportunity, not a fate; an enrichment, not a diminishment. It is a beginning, no less challenging because it is the beginning of an end. I think of another Saul, who later became Paul. His life was crowned with service to the very end. His epitaph might have been, "I have fought the good fight, I have finished the race, I have kept the faith" (2 Tim. 4:7, RSV). To his final breath, he pressed on for the upward calling of God in Christ Jesus. That is the spirit every retired person needs when others look on him or her as a "used-to-be."

Prayer: God of the morning, noon, and evening of life: Help us to find new challenges and joys in our retired years with the confidence that "He who began a good work in us will bring it to completion at the day of Jesus Christ." Amen.[2]

For Discussion and Reflection

1. Was there a transition you experienced earlier in life that made you rethink your identity, and if so, did you find anything particularly helpful in developing a new way of thinking of yourself? (This could have been when changing jobs, getting married or divorced, experiencing an empty nest, or moving to a new city.)

2. Richard Morgan points to another example of a person having a changed name and direction, Saul who became the apostle

Paul. What can we learn from his experience and his dedication in the remainder of his life to "forgetting what lies behind and reaching forward to what lies ahead . . . [pressing] on toward the goal for the prize of the upward call of God in Christ Jesus" (Phil. 3:13–14, NASB)?

Witness of Scripture: New Identities

The Scripture gives us wonderful examples of individuals receiving a new name, and with it new hope and new purpose. For example, Genesis 17:1–6 is a remarkable story of God's unfolding work in history through the first patriarch. We first encounter this man as Abram in Genesis 12. In this context God calls him from his ancestral home to journey forth to Canaan at age seventy-five. Now, in Genesis 17, Abram is commissioned (at age ninety-nine) to be the "ancestor of a multitude of nations" and his name is changed to Abraham (vv. 4–5). And in the New Testament Jesus changes Simon's name to Cephas or Peter, commissioning him to be the rock among the disciples (John 1:42). As we have seen, Richard Morgan mentions a man named Saul from Tarsus who takes on a new name and identity as the great apostle Paul.

This same apostle proclaimed that all of us have a new identity in Christ. We are all "children of God" whether "Jew or Greek . . . slave or free . . . male or female . . . " (Gal. 3:26, 28). Our identity does not rest on what we do or on our status in the world but in our relationship to the One who calls us into the fullness of our humanity. For the early Christ-followers, this was startlingly good news, a surprising gift especially for those on the bottom of the social hierarchy. It is similarly good news for us today, especially in times of transition and loss when we wonder who we are. Now we begin to see *whose* we are, and through the grace of God claim our greatest identity.

For Discussion and Reflection

1. What kind of new identity, hope, or purpose do you see being given Abraham, Jeremiah, or Peter in the passages noted?

2. Is there a new or altered identity or purpose for you in retirement? Who would you like to become?

The Practice of Spiritual Reading

While a number of practices contribute to our understanding of who we are in retirement, the practice of spiritual reading can play a particularly important role in our understanding and refining our identity in this phase of life.

What is spiritual reading? The term relates to *what* we read as well as *how* we read it. Spiritual literature includes the Bible of course. Other books to enrich our spiritual life include spiritual classics such as Augustine's *Confessions,* Benedict's *Rule,* John Bunyan's *Pilgrim's Progress,* John Wesley's *Journal,* Teresa of Avila's *Interior Castle,* and Thomas à Kempis's *Imitation of Christ.* These titles and many more Christian spiritual classics are available through such publishers as Paraclete, Renovare and Paulist Press.

Spiritual reading also refers to *how* we read. New Testament scholar Bob Mulholland contrasts reading for *information* (what we do most of the time) and reading for *formation.*[3] When we read for information speed is of the essence. The goal is to gather facts, ideas, and opinions as fast as we can. In reading for *formation* we read to be shaped by what we read. Less is more and so we read slowly, meditatively, perhaps spending an hour on a single sentence so that we might fully receive what it has to say to us.

The term used for this meditative reading is *lectio divina* (Latin for "divine reading"). Developed by the Benedictines in the sixth century, the practice typically takes a few verses of Scripture or a single verse, reading first for familiarity and then for prayer and contemplation. Reflecting on the passage from Hebrews in which the Scripture is spoken of as "living and active, sharper than a two-edged sword, . . . able to judge the thoughts and intentions of the heart" (Heb. 4:12–13), Marjorie J. Thompson notes that in spiritual reading "it is not so much we who read the Word as the Word who reads us."[4] Or in the words of Paul, it is the practice by which we learn and adopt the mind of Christ (Phil. 2:5) and are "equipped for every good work" (2 Tim. 3:16–17).

Recent interest in recovering the practice of *lectio divina* has resulted in some excellent resources describing the practice more fully, including that by Norvene Vest for small group gatherings.[5] *The Meeting God Bible* suggests numerous "entry points" for the meditative reading of Scripture; it's available in both NRSV and NIV translations.[6]

12 Looking to the Future with Hope

When we wrote our first book, *Shaping a Life of Significance for Retirement,* we focused primarily on the years just prior to and shortly after retirement. Yet, often we heard that it was not only the here and now that preoccupied the soon-to-be retired and those in the early phases of adjustment. Many retirees live with a keen awareness of a future that seems limited and uncertain. We've heard two important realities mentioned repeatedly. The first is the need to plan for the later stages of life, when our physical capabilities are not be what they are today. And the second is the firm commitment to hope and a willingness to live each day fully with gratitude and trust.

Experience of Retirees

Sister Joan *(Franciscan sister who prior to her retirement served as head of the school system for a Diocese of the Roman Catholic Church)*

Life, in every stage, has called me to look to the future. Though I may not have realized it at the time, it was a reflective moment on the future that usually initiated my taking concrete steps of planning whether for short-term or long-term spans of my life.

Since I have come to live in a retirement home, planning for the future has taken on a much more focused faith-life component. The reflective moment has become a way of life for me. Daily I am aware that *time* is my future as it always has been. The same questions come to me: Who am I? Who am I becoming? My faith life tells me that I am a valuable person, a child of God who is loved unconditionally by a merciful God.

In prayer and personal reflection, I recognize that this journey with myself brings me face to face with the person I really am. I came letting go of things—closeness to family and friends, a home, familiar situations, a ministry I loved, a place I loved to be, a part of life I didn't want to lose, all aspects of my life with which I could be identified. I spent time recalling these good times as I moved into the future. It is heartwarming to reminisce and tell my story of the past and remember the good. Even repeating some of the feelings during struggles and the lessons learned from the hard times is comforting.

The challenge for me has been to replace the sense of letting go with the attitude of embracing the life in me, gifts of person that have not changed, and the new opportunities for life fulfillment. Since I do not know how, what, or when these opportunities for living a full life will come to me, I begin each day with prayer that my eyes, mind, and spirit will be ready.

A friend of mine died recently from ALS. I played Scrabble with her on Thanksgiving Day. As she struggled to say the word she wanted and I struggled to hear it, we saw in each other's eyes amusement and satisfaction when it was on the board. She was younger than I, but shared in her last months what it means to live fully in the present that leads to the future. Her joyful spirit will live in my heart far into my future.

The task of looking to the future for me, a retired person, moves me from the letting go experienced during the pre-retirement and moving phase to the *embracing* of the joys and struggles of the closing phase of my life. The role model I need to recognize first is that of myself. If I am to love my neighbor as myself, then I must love all that is *me*, and be willing to share myself with others. The spiritual challenge I am facing now is learning to *embrace* my life here and be willing to share the depths of my soul. I recognize the value of telling my story as I am living it now, and listening to the wisdom of those around me who are also living into their future, our future.

For Discussion and Reflection

1. As you read Sister Joan's reflections on leaving behind a role she loved and her orientation toward embracing the joys and the struggles of the last phase of life, what attitudes and actions do you see in her that may be important for you?

2. Sister Joan is among those we have met who look at entering a continuous care facility as a real ministry. Can you envision this for yourself, and if so what might be your unique contribution?

3. Are there steps that might be wise for you to take at this point to begin to understand your options for living in the later stages of your life?

Witness of Scripture: Planning and Hope

Sister Joan's account highlights both the importance of proactively planning for this phase of life and embracing its joys and challenges with real hope. Her approach to this phase of life personifies the reality of the Old Testament book of Proverbs. Proverbs 21:5, for example, points out that "the plans of the diligent lead surely to abundance, but everyone who is hasty comes only to want." And Proverbs 16:3 says to "commit your work to the Lord, and your plans will be established."

The words of Paul are also relevant in this context: "We also boast in our sufferings, knowing that suffering produces endurance, and endurance produces character, and character produces hope, and hope does not disappoint us, because God's love has been poured into our hearts through the Holy Spirit that has been given to us" (Rom. 5:3–5).

In Scripture hope is not pie-in-the-sky denial of the harsh realities of life. Jeremiah looked at the pending doom of foreign invasion and proclaimed the assurance that God will offer "a future with hope" (Jer. 29:11). He even bought land when the country was under siege (Jer. 32:1–8). And when the early Church was sorely afflicted, persecuted, and about to lose its way, Peter proclaimed that it would be "a living hope" and a "holy nation" (1 Pet. 1:3, 2:9). During the season of Advent, and always, we wait in hope, knowing that the world is still in darkness, knowing the reality of suffering and death perhaps more clearly than ever before, but hearing also with Mary the angel's song that "nothing will be impossible with God" (Luke 1:37).

For followers of Jesus Christ to be realistic is to have hope, for hope is embedded in the fabric of God's reality. This does not mean hope is easy to find in the midst of society's neglect of children, for example, and the intransigent dynamics of global conflict. Sometimes we have to look pretty hard. Yet hope is there, for Christ is there, and in him we find strength for the day. This beautiful benediction appears in the New Testament: "Now may our Lord Jesus Christ himself and God our Father, who loved us and through grace gave us eternal comfort and good hope, comfort your hearts and strengthen them in every good work and word" (2 Thess. 2:16–17).

For Discussion and Reflection

1. We may be tempted at times to think that planning and faith are incompatible. Do God and planning seem disconnected in Proverbs 16:3 and 21:5, or is a different understanding suggested?

2. How do you see the reality of hope manifested in Sister Joan's description of the current stage of her life? What could the implications be of your living with a more hopeful orientation?

Anxiety robs us of our capacity to live in the present. And it makes it hard for us to look to the future with hope. Anxiety destroys our prayer life and disrupts our interpersonal relationships as well; it can even affect us physically. Thanks to biofeedback and relaxation techniques, we now have ways to lower anxiety apart from drugs. These techniques (which reflect ancient spiritual traditions) can also help us develop a practice of prayer that may lead to a healthier and more centered way of being in the world.

One of the authors (Jerry) has developed a practice for nonanxious praying, incorporating ideas from several sources.[1] Here is a description of his practice, which you may wish to try.

After spending about ten minutes in spiritual reading, put your Bible and prayer book aside and commit to twenty minutes for silent reflection. Begin by simply letting your mind and body rest in the Presence of the Loving God. Breathe deeply and gently, relaxing your stomach so that the air can enter the lower parts of your lungs. Let go of what you've read; most of the words and phrases will be forgotten and that's okay. Instead, linger over whatever sense of God's Presence you now feel as you enter into the silence.

Shift your focus to your body. Your physical body is a gift from God, a sensitive and valuable instrument for perceiving and interacting with the world. Inhale gently and deeply and hold your breath for a few seconds, letting your stomach expand so that the lower recesses of your lungs can fill with air; then exhale slowly and completely. Repeat several times. Feel your body relaxing as the air fills the recesses of your lungs. The Scripture word for "breath" is the same as the word for "spirit" (Hebrew: *ruach;* Greek: *pnuema*). By breathing deeply we are literally "in-spirited" or "inspired." As you continue to breathe slowly, let go of any tension or stress or pain you feel in your body. Repeat several times if you wish until you have reached a deeper level of relaxation.

You live in the world of time, which can cause much anxiety. We don't feel we have enough time or we don't know what to do with the time we have or we have regrets. Continue to breathe deeply and relax as you reflect on the last few days or the next few days. If you feel uneasy about a conversation that you had yesterday, acknowledge the feeling and let it go. If you're anxious about a meeting coming up, do the same. Let it go and relax. God has given you this time to be in God's Presence, so be present to God's peace and love here and now.

Now focus just on today. God wants you to be present to this day. Of all the things you need to focus on, what is the one thing that needs your full attention, your energy, your time? Relax as you think of the priority for the day. You may recall something that you read before this time of silent meditation that will help you, something from Scripture or your prayer book. Or perhaps some other encouragement comes to mind: a friend, a good memory, the sense of satisfaction when the task is done. This is what it means to live by the Spirit: living in the here and now of God's Presence.

As this time of silent meditation comes to a close, know that God loves you very much. Offer a prayer of thanks and go forward into the day.

13 Closing Comments

Life beyond full-time work involves a set of personal transitions and also presents us with unique opportunities and challenges. We believe it can also be a spiritual pilgrimage, a unique time in one's life to deepen one's relationship with God, with others and with the world around us. In this book we have offered personal examples, reflections on Scripture, and suggested spiritual practices to encourage you on your sacred journey through this phase of life. The real work, and fun, of confronting these personal dimensions of retirement continues as we bring them to bear on our own life circumstances, interests, and strengths.

We also recognize that circumstances and concerns at any point in pre-retirement or retirement change with the passing of time. Both of us have experienced this reality and found it necessary to rethink various areas of transition, opportunity, and challenge. For example, both of us have found it necessary to revisit the portfolio of activities we initially "retired to." An important part of what Jack initially "retired to" was frequent interaction with young grandchildren. And another element was a fairly busy consulting schedule. But the grandchildren have grown toward independence in the intervening eight years; and the duration of the consulting commitments has decreased.

While Jack was semi-retired when we published our first book, Jerry was still working full-time. Even though he had heard many of the stories of what others experienced as they entered retirement, he found the transition more challenging than he had imagined. He found it hard to slow down. He quickly became involved in a number of non-profit organizations, volunteered to teach in his church and in the community, and served as leader for several special projects. Now, however, he has begun balancing his "portfolio" with more time for family, better self-care, reading and travel. In this new phase of retirement, he feels a "tug" for a more contemplative lifestyle, a time to grow closer to God and others.

Both of us continue to seek to understand this time in our life as spiritual pilgrimage. We seek the guidance of Scripture, engage in regular spiritual practices and enjoy good Christian friends (as well as non-Christian friends). We have experienced surprising grace and much love, even during the difficult times. We have also felt that the readings and practices we have offered in this book barely scratch the surface of the potential of what is available. The Christian faith is a very rich and life-giving tradition. Scripture and the variety of spiritual practices are vast resources. New and lifelong friendships hold us accountable and make us laugh when we take ourselves too seriously. Listening keenly to others in their journey as well as telling our story are two practices which build strong bonds of agape love.

We encourage you to see this time of your life as spiritual pilgrimage also. Jane Marie Thibault suggests that this phase of life can be "a deepening love affair" with God.[1] As we grow older, we can grow closer to God, to others and to our true identity with Christ. Far from being drudgery, this life with God can be the greatest adventure of all.

Appendix A Sample Session for Covenant Group

As noted in the introduction, *Retirement as Spiritual Pilgrimage* is a faith resource that may be used by itself or in combination with our earlier book, *Shaping a Life of Significance for Retirement.* The earlier book identifies key personal transitions, opportunities, and challenges associated with entering into and living life beyond full-time work. *Retirement as Spiritual Pilgrimage* builds on this knowledge base and seeks to offer spiritual guidance through these personal transitions, opportunities, and challenges by sharing experiences of individual retirees, listening to Scripture, and suggesting spiritual practices.

This book offers a rich resource for small groups. We suggest two models: an adult Sunday school class (as described in appendix B) and a covenant group (which we describe here). Rather than a session-by-session guide, we discuss the basis for deciding what kind of group you want to initiate and provide a detailed plan for the first session of a covenant group (based on chapter 1) in this appendix. Then, in appendix B, we provide the outline for a Sunday school class (based on chapter 2). You'll then have the opportunity to develop further sessions according to your instincts as a leader and the group's response.

Covenant Group or Adult Sunday School Class: What's the Difference?

Over the last forty years, a variety of small group models have been developed for adult learning and Christian formation. The covenant group is one of these and may be best understood in contrast to the adult Sunday school class. Typically, adult Sunday school classes meet at an appointed time in a classroom setting, gathering around a book or curriculum, led by a capable leader. While many members of the class may attend every Sunday, visitors are welcome at any time. A typical class session includes substantial input by the leader, with some time for prayer, discussion, and sharing. Because the focus is primarily on the teaching itself, the size of an adult Sunday school class can vary from three or four to forty or more. As a practical matter, the Sunday school hour is often much less than sixty minutes—enough time to deliver the content of the material but not to process it individually or as a group.

In contrast, covenant groups often meet during the week for an hour and a half or more. The purpose of the covenant group is to provide a safe space for participants to process (reflect, integrate, and try out) what they are learning. The role of the leader shifts from teacher to facilitator, guide, and timekeeper. Group size is limited to twelve or less, with the optimal size between six and ten. A primary feature of the covenant group is confidentiality; what is shared in the group, stays in the group. Because of this feature, drop-in participation is not allowed. Once a group starts, participation is established and those wanting to join are encouraged to wait until another group begins. A key for having a good covenant group experience is the mutual desire to follow a set of behavior guidelines. We particularly recommend the guidelines found in the Upper Room's *Companions in Christ* series, reprinted here:

- Speak only for yourself about beliefs, feelings, and responses.

- Respect and receive what others offer, even if you disagree.

- Listening is more important than talking. Avoid crosstalk, interrupting, speaking for others, or trying to "fix" another person's problems.

- Honor the different ways God works in individuals.

- Do not be afraid of silence. Use it to listen to the Spirit in your midst.

- Maintain confidentiality. What is shared in the group stays in the group.

- Recognize that all group members have permission to pass, sharing only when they are ready.[1]

Additional insights about covenant groups are included in the *Companions in Christ* series. Leading such groups requires a capacity to establish trust as well as boundaries. Covenant groups are not therapy groups though sometimes deep healing does occur. Personal sharing is encouraged with the focus on the movement of the Spirit in our life, not on deep-seated problems or unresolved conflicts. Lighting a candle, beginning with silence and including time for individual reflection as well as group sharing help the group have a balanced approach.

How Many Sessions?

To organize a covenant group, we suggest an informal introductory session to acquaint people with *Retiring as Spiritual Pilgrimage* and chart a plan. Here you can describe how such groups function, talk about why they can be so valuable, and answer any questions potential participants might have. Not everyone is ready or wants to participate in a covenant group, so this is a good time to clarify intentions. If there are people who seem interested and ready, consider inviting them to the first session. If it's really not a good fit, assure them they can withdraw. Actually experiencing a covenant group dispels a lot of fear and anxiety.

When will you meet and for how long? We suggest one to one-and-one-half hours and an initial agreement to meet six times. Have the group meet around the first four chapters of *Retirement as Spiritual Pilgrimage* ("Beginning the Journey,", "Living with Meaning in a Smaller World," "Retirement and Family Relationships," and "Retirement and Friendship"). Look over the remaining eight chapters and decide which ones you want to offer to the group, and then talk with them about your selections to see if the topics fit with the group's interest. A younger group may be less interested in discussing declining physical capacity or mortality, though the opposite might be the case as well. Before session six, decide as a group if you want to continue to meet for two, four, or six more sessions around the remaining topics.

As the group's convener, your primary role is to facilitate the group's process. You do this by modeling open, honest sharing as a norm for the group; by respecting their boundaries; by holding them accountable to the guidelines (from *Companions in Christ* above) so group members aren't trying to fix one another, for example; and by keeping the group on time. Often the facilitator's role is simply to affirm the group when things go well and gently guide them back to a more loving path when they need it.

You may want to recruit a member of the group to present the input for each gathering. For example, for session one this person would read chapter 1 ("Beginning the Journey"), study the suggested Scriptures, and then summarize the content for the group in the five minutes allotted. That way leadership is shared, the content is summarized for anyone who failed to read it, and you can be free to facilitate the process rather than serve as the authority on the topic.

Session Outline

Before the group arrives

Ask everyone to read chapter 1, "Beginning the Journey." Encourage them to jot down their responses to the questions at the end of the personal accounts and Scripture meditation. Copies of the book *Shaping a Life of Significance for Retirement* may be of interest for those who want to do further reading on the personal dimensions of retirement. Be sure to have paper, pens, and nametags as well. Bring a candle and a lighter and copies of the *Upper Room Worship book* if available.[2] Print copies of the guidelines from *Companions in Christ* (above) for everyone.

Arrange for a meeting space that is comfortable and casual, with softer lights and a more relaxed setting, no tables or podiums, with chairs arranged in a circle. Place a candle in the center of the group as a reminder of the light of Christ guiding us through every transition in our lives. For this first session, you may want to add visual reminders of a journey: sandals, a map, a walking stick or staff. Say a prayer for those who are coming.

Welcome and Opening (10 minutes)

Welcome people in a casual and relaxed way. Start the group on time by inviting them to be seated. Let them know you are glad that they are here and that you are looking forward to meeting together for these six sessions as a small group. Share your own excitement and interest in discovering what God will reveal during your time together. Then in silence light the candle as a sign of Christ's presence. After another minute of silence, offer a brief prayer for the time you have together for this session. Invite them to join in singing #109 in the *Upper Room Worship Book* ("Traveling with God" by Sydney Carter) or some other hymn/song with a strong journey motif.[3]

After the song, hand out copies of the guidelines from *Companions in Christ* and talk about what it means to be a part of a covenant group. Let participants know that you are hoping they will come to all six sessions. If some are coming to this first session to try it out, be sure to comment on this. Ask participants to let you know if they are planning to continue with the group or not. Take time for any questions and deal with them as a group.

Introduce the Theme (5 minutes)

Briefly say a few words about the theme for this session, "Beginning the Journey." If you have recruited someone to summarize this chapter, ask them to do so now. Be sure they refer to the Scripture passage (Gen. 12:1–4). Here they may add a brief word about who Abram was and the role he played in Israel's history.

Exploring the Theme in Dyads (Twosomes) (15 minutes)

Ask the participants to pair up to reflect on the meditation by Sharon ("Experience of Retirees" in chapter 1 above). Have them share their responses to the three questions at the end of the article. Halfway through (at seven-and-a-half minutes) ring a bell to let them know that if only one person has been talking, it's time for that person to listen.

De-briefing as Total Group (5 minutes)

Re-assemble as a total group and invite people to share their responses to any of the three questions. Does the analogy of a journey make sense as a way of understanding retirement?

Break (5 minutes)

Telling Your Story—Preparation (15 minutes)

Invite each person to look over the section on that practice in chapter 1. Remind them of the value of telling their story as a way to gain perspective and insight on their experience, on themselves and on God's presence on their journey. It is also important to tell people that stories are dynamic; they change as we change. Details that are vivid at first fade and diminish in importance. Time may help us to see our story more clearly, and it may help us understand God's work in our lives in a different way.

In preparation for telling the story of your retirement journey so far to two other persons in our group, have each person write his or her responses to the questions posed at the end of the section in chapter 1 on "Telling Your Story." Ask the group to work in silence on their individual responses.

Telling Your Story—Triads (25 minutes)

Based on what you know about the participants so far, we recommend that you assign people to groups of three, balancing out personalities and histories. For this exercise, it's best if good friends and spouses are in separate groups. Explain that each participant will have a role: presenter, listener, or observer. The presenter has eight minutes to tell his or her story. The listener has a minute to ask a question or two for clarification. The observer invites the group into a minute of silent prayer before moving on to the next presenter. For the second time around, the listener becomes the presenter, the observer becomes the listener, and the presenter becomes the observer. The pattern is repeated a third time so that all have had a chance to tell their story.

At the end of twenty minutes, call time and ask the triad to debrief their experience. Remind the group about the guidelines, suggesting that this is not a time to fix someone. Ask them to close their time together with prayer

Debriefing as Total Group (5 minutes)

Welcome the participants back together as a total group. Invite them to share their feelings about what this experience was like (but not the content or details of what was shared). Was it hard to tell their story in only eight minutes? Was it helpful to focus in such a concentrated way? What surprised you in this process, either as listener, presenter, or observer?

Closing Worship and Assignments for Next Time (5 minutes)

Join in singing again the song you used at the beginning. Remind the group to read chapter 2 of *Retirement as Spiritual Pilgrimage* (You may also recommend that they read chapter 1 of *Shaping a Life of Significance for Retirement* if this earlier book is being used as an additional resource). Gather in a circle for prayer such as this one from Richard Morgan:

"Eternal Keeper: Retirement is a moment of transition on Life's journey. We take courage in the knowledge that you are our Keeper and will watch over our coming and going both now and forevermore. Amen."[4]

End with the Lord's Prayer. As people are leaving, be sure to check with anyone who might have come simply to check out the group to see if they have decided to continue with the group.

Appendix B Sample Session for Adult Sunday School Class

An adult Sunday school class has both important advantages and challenges compared to a smaller and more intimate covenant group setting. A key advantage is that Sunday school attracts a broad range of adult participants. It thereby offers a real opportunity to introduce the topic of life beyond full-time work to a significant number of pre-retirees and retirees in a congregation. The corresponding limitations relative to a midweek small group are less time in each session (typically forty-five minutes or less) and less consistency in attendance from one Sunday to the next. Nevertheless, our experience with the materials in *Retirement as Spiritual Pilgrimage* (as well as with *Shaping a Life of Significance for Retirement*) in the adult Sunday school context convinces us that they can be used as the basis for a meaningful series for your class.

In appendix A, we offered a discussion of the differences between covenant groups and adult Sunday school classes and an outline for a covenant group focusing on chapter 1 of this book. In preparing to use Retirement as a Spiritual Pilgrimage for an adult Sunday school series, we suggest that you review the content of appendix A as well as this appendix, in which we offer a suggested outline for a Sunday school class for chapter 2 ("Living with Meaning in the Smaller World of Retirement"). As the leader of an adult Sunday school class you face some of the same challenges as a small group leader, particularly in terms of the gauging the orientation and makeup of your class. If, for example, you have participants that are primarily approaching and in the early stages of retirement, you may wish to emphasize the first nine chapters of this book, with one session per chapter. If you have a more diverse group, the book can be used as the basis for a thirteen-week series.

The fundamental difference between what we suggest by way of a session outline for your class context and for the covenant group derives from the difference in time available in the two cases. Our overall suggestion is to concentrate class time reflecting on the personal account of the retiree or retirees and on the Scripture reflection for the chapter you are covering. Then point to the spiritual practice as the practical application and encourage each class member to consider how to incorporate this into his or her life in the coming week.

Purpose of the Session on Living in a Smaller World in Retirement

This session serves to explore in more depth the experience of moving from a larger world of influence, authority, or recognition in full-time work to a smaller world of one or more of those things in retirement. Additionally, the participants will begin to recognize life beyond full-time work as a part of one's spiritual journey, a time of growth in one's relationship to Christ.

Before the Group Arrives

Ask everyone to read chapter 2 of *Retirement as Spiritual Pilgrimage*. (Also have them read the introduction and chapter 1 of *Shaping a Life of Significance in Retirement* if using this resource as a companion in the study.) Encourage them to jot down their responses to the questions at the end of the Witness of Scripture section of Chapter 2. Be sure to have paper, pens, and nametags as well.

Welcome and Opening (10 minutes)

Welcome people in a casual and relaxed way, and encourage an atmosphere of give-and-take by having chairs arranged in a semicircle.

Invite people to share their names and a little of why they have come. Alternatively, ask each person the question, what is one thing your parents did well in retirement? This question often leads to a lively and productive discussion.

Discussion of Personal Account (10 minutes)

Invite participants to share their impressions of Brenda's account of leaving teaching (Experience of Retirees section of chapter 2). Point out that this feeling of going from a larger to a smaller world was common in the interviews, and pose the question following Brenda's account for group discussion. (Additional discussion questions for your consideration are listed at the end of chapter 1 of *Shaping a Life of Significance for Retirement*.)

Scripture Meditation (15 minutes)

Read Galatians 1:16–21 as a group. Pose for group discussion the question at the end of the Witness of Scripture section of chapter 2.

Practical Application (5 minutes)

Point out that one practical application of this session is to adopt the spiritual practice of letting go, discussed in chapter 2. To this end encourage each person, either on their own or better with another class member to discuss this question during the week: What is one value or practice that you feel will be particularly important and challenging for you to let go of as you move from full-time work to whatever follows? Or if already retired, ask, Is there an area that you have already found important to consciously let go of?

Prepare for Next Time and Closing (5 minutes)

Ask the group to read chapter 3 of *Retirement as Spiritual Pilgrimage*. (You may also suggest chapter 2 of *Shaping a Life of Significance* to those who are interested in additional background on the topic of the next session.) Encourage them to ponder the questions posed in chapter 3 and write their responses in their journal.

Close with prayer, asking God to guide each person's thinking about what he or she needs to let go of to be all that they can beyond full-time work.

Appendix C Suggested Ritual for

Honoring Retirees

The transition from full-time work to whatever follows, whether it is retirement, semi-retirement, or new employment, can be a significant event in a person's life. Recognizing the importance of this passage is one of the ways for the church to show its support. As with other life transitions, here the church can offer the ministry of the gospel, with prayers of gratitude for what is past and prayers of discernment for God's call now.

In preparation for this ritual, the pastor or volunteer is encouraged to talk with the persons retiring about their work and about the transitions they are making. Helpful questions for this discussion can be found in appendix B of *Shaping a Life of Significance for Retirement*. The persons retiring should be encouraged to ponder how God might be guiding them now in their retirement and how their retirement might be a time for deepening their discipleship and service to others. As an alternative to the one-on-one approach, those retiring might be gathered together as a group for conversation regarding this important transition and a ritual like the one below offered for all those retiring in a particular year. This ritual could be offered as a part of Sunday morning worship or at a Sunday school class or social gathering at the church.

A Ritual for Those Who Are Retiring

After gathering the retiree(s) before the congregation, the pastor or other leader identifies the significance of this event with these or similar words:

Pastor: As followers of Jesus Christ, we know that Christ is present to us every day of our lives, when we worship and when we work, in ordinary moments, and in the special events of our lives. So now we celebrate Christ's presence here on this occasion as we recognize those who are retiring from careers that have shaped their lives in significant ways.

In your baptism you were marked as a Christian disciple and given a new identity as a beloved Child of God. As you retire, I invite you to remember your baptism and be thankful.

The pastor may invite each retiree to touch the waters of baptism in font or bowl as a remembrance of God's grace and call.

Pastor: As Christ-followers, we are given a vocation to live out the gospel whatever our life circumstance, whether employed or unemployed, whether young or old, whether able-bodied or no longer able-bodied. All of us are called to remember the Great Commandment: to love God and neighbor in all that we do. As you retire from your working career, I invite you to remember the lifelong vocation to which we are all called through the gospel of Jesus Christ.

The pastor may raise the Bible as sign of our lifelong vocation in Christ. An appropriate Scripture such as Philippians 1:3–11 or 3:10–14 may be read by the pastor or by one of those retiring.

Pastor: As followers of the Way, we affirm life as a spiritual journey, beginning at birth and continuing throughout our lives with family, friends, Christian community, and careers that sometimes challenge us and sometimes bring great fulfillment. As you retire, what word of celebration, gratitude, relief, or wisdom do you have to share?

Here those retiring may be invited to share a few words before the pastor concludes.

Pastor: In the days and weeks to come, as you begin this new phase in your life, we encourage you to celebrate all that is past and to seek God's guidance in the here and now. In your retirement you may receive a new and surprising invitation from God to grow spiritually, come closer to your family, celebrate friendships old and new, offer care to others, serve those in need, and to change the world.

However God calls you, know that you are loved by God and by this community of _____church.

> *Here those retiring may be invited to kneel and the pastor may offer a prayer of guidance for their new life as retirees. At the end of the prayer, as a sign of their new beginning in Christ, retirees may be invited to light a candle on the altar as a dedication and celebration of all that they have accomplished and may be called to do today.*

Notes

INTRODUCTION

1. R. Jack Hansen and Jerry P. Haas, *Shaping a Life of Significance for Retirement* (Nashville, TN: Upper Room Books, 2010).

2. Joan Chittister, *The Gift of Years: Growing Old Gracefully* (New York: Blue Bridge Books, 2008).

CHAPTER 1

1. The practice of telling one's story in the context of God's work in our lives is also called witnessing. See Dorothy C. Bass, ed., *Practicing our Faith: A Way of Life for a Searching People* (San Francisco: Jossey-Bass, 1997). Richard L. Morgan's book *Remembering Your Story: Creating Your Own Spiritual Autobiography*, rev. ed. (Nashville, TN: Upper Room Books, 2002) offers a complete workbook and small group resource for developing this practice

CHAPTER 2

1. Joyce Rupp, *Little Pieces of Light . . . : Darkness and Personal Growth* (Mahwah, NJ: Paulist Press, 1994), 10

2. Linda Douty, *How Can I Let Go If I Don't Know I'm Holding On: Setting Our Souls Free* (Harrisburg, PA: Morehouse Publishing, 2005), 41

3. Loretta L. Marshall, *The Upper Room Disciplines* (Nashville, TN: Upper Room Books, 2010), 354.

CHAPTER 3

1. Lillian S. Hawthorne, *Sisters and Brothers All These Years: Taking Another Look at the Longest Relationship in Your Life* (Acton, MA: Vanderwyk and Burnham, 2003).

2. Dave Isay, ed., *Listening Is an Act of Love* (New York: The Penguin Press, 2007).

CHAPTER 4

1. yquotes.com (http://yquotes.com/quotes/phillips-brooks/)

2. Aelred of Rievaulx, *Spiritual Friendship,* trans. Mary Eugenia Laker SSND (Kalamazoo, MI: Cistercian Publications, 1977).

3. C. S. Lewis, *The Four Loves* (New York and London: Harcourt Brace Jovanovich, 1960), 87–127.

CHAPTER 5

1. Hansen and Haas, *Shaping a Life of Significance for Retirement,* chapter 4, Retiring to as Well as from Something, 42-48.

2. Merriam-Webster online (http://www.merriam-webster.com/dictionary/discern)

3. Parker J. Palmer, *A Hidden Wholeness: The Journey Toward an Undivided Life* (San Francisco: Jossey-Bass, 2004). For a small group resource on discernment, see *The Way of Discernment* by Stephen V. Doughty and Marjorie J. Thompson (Nashville, TN: Upper Room Books, 2008). A participant's book and a leader's guide are available. This resource includes an extensive bibliography on the topic of discernment.

CHAPTER 6

1. Wayne A. Meeks, *The First Urban Christians: The Social World of the Apostle Paul* (New Haven, CT: Yale University Press, 1983).

2. Karla M. Kincannon, *Creativity and Divine Surprise: Finding the Place of Your Resurrection* (Nashville, TN: Upper Room Books, 2005), prologue, Kindle edition, no pagination.

3. Julia Cameron, *The Artist's Way: A Spiritual Path to Higher Creativity* (New York: Putnam, 1992). Buzz's writing resulted in a book, *Running Deep with Strangers: A Must for Human Survival* (no publisher or date listed; ISBN 978-1-5029-1459-0).

4. See for example Howard Gardner, *Multiple Intelligences: New Horizons in Theory and Practice* (New York: Basic Books, 2008).

5. Kincannon, *Creativity and Divine Surprise,* "Invitation."

6. Kincannon, *Creativity and Divine Surprise,* "Prologue."

CHAPTER 7

1. Gail Sheehy, *New Passages: Mapping Your Life Across Time* (New York: Ballantine Books, 1995).

2. Abigail Trafford, *My Time: Making the Most of the Bonus Decades after Fifty* (New York: Basic Books, 2004).

3. Joseph D. Driskill, *Protestant Spiritual Exercises* (Harrisburg, PA: Morehouse Publishing, 1999),49.

4. Hansen and Haas, *Shaping a Life of Significance for Retirement,* chapter 5, Growing Spiritually and Intellectually, 49-53.

5. NOMADS is organized by the General Board of Global Ministries, an agency of the United Methodist Church. NOMADS stands for "**N**omads **O**n a **M**ission **A**ctive in **D**ivine **S**ervice." More information can be found at http://www.nomadsumc.org/

CHAPTER 8

1. More discussion of the variety of caregiving responsibilities in retirement is provided in Hansen and Haas, *Shaping a Life of Significance for Retirement,* chapter 6, Responding to the Call of Caregiving, 55-59.

2. When the authors conducted a survey of retirees, about a third were involved in caregiving for a family member. Several described the feelings reported here. See *Shaping a Life of Significance for Retirement,* chapter 6, Responding to the Call of Caregiving, 55-59.

3. Marjorie J. Thompson, *Soul Feast: An Invitation to the Christian Spiritual Life* (Louisville, KY: Westminster John Knox Press, 1995).

4. Nell E. Noonan, *Not Alone: Encouragement for Caregivers* (Nashville, TN: Upper Room Books, 2009).

5. *The Upper Room* published bimonthly by The Upper Room, Inc., a ministry of The United Methodist Church's Discipleship Ministries, Nashville, TN, http://devotional.upperroom.org/

CHAPTER 9

1. Hansen and Haas, *Shaping a Life of Significance for Retirement,* chapter 8, Meeting declines in Physical Capabilities, 69.

2. Ernest Becker, *The Denial of Death* (New York: Free Press, 1997).

3. Huston Smith with Jeffery Paine, *Tales of Wonder: Adventures Chasing the Divine, an Autobiography* (New York: Harper Collins, 2009), 180

CHAPTER 10

1. Hansen and Haas, *Shaping a Life of Significance for Retirement,* chapter 9, We Won't Live Forever, 73-76.

2. N. T. Wright, *Surprised by Hope: Rethinking Heaven, the Resurrection, and the Mission of the Church* (New York: Harper Collins, 2008).

3. Henri J. M. Nouwen, Michael J. Christensen, and Rebecca J. Laird, *Spiritual Formation: Following the Movements of the Spirit* (New York: HarperOne, 2010).

4. Isaac Watts, 1719, "I'll Praise My Maker While I've Breath," alt. by John Wesley 1737, *The United Methodist Hymnal* (Nashville, TN: The United Methodist Publishing House, 1964), #60.

CHAPTER 11

1. Richard L. Morgan, *I Never Found That Rocking Chair: God's Call at Retirement* (Nashville, TN: Upper Room Books, 1992), o.p. This book has been reprinted as *Beyond the Rocking Chair: God's Call at Retirement* (Eugene, OR: Wipf and Stock, 2009).

2. Morgan, "Used-to-Beism," meditation #35 in *I Never Found That Rocking Chair: God's Call at Retirement,* © Richard Morgan. . Used with the author's permission.

3. Robert Mulholland Jr., *Shaped by the Word: The Power of Scripture in Spiritual Formation,* 2nd ed. (Nashville, TN: Upper Room Books, 2001).

4. Thompson, *Soul Feast,* 20.

5. Norvene Vest, *Gathered in the Word: Praying the Scripture in Small Groups* (Nashville, TN: Upper Room Books, 1996).

6. Timothy Jones, ed., *The Meeting God Bible: Growing in Intimacy with God through Scripture* (Nashville, TN: Upper Room Books, 2009).

CHAPTER 12

1. See for example Flora Slosson Wuellner's *Prayer, Stress, and Our Inner Wounds* (Upper Room Books, Nashville, TN, 1985). See also resources related to the practice of lectio divina, Scripture meditation, such as references 3 and 5 for chapter 11 above.

CHAPTER 13 CLOSING COMMENTS

1. A Deepening Love Affair: The Gift of God in Later Life by Jane Marie Thibault (Upper Room Books, Nashville, TN, 1993).

1. From *Companions in Christ: A Small-Group Experience in Spiritual Formation, Leader's Guide* (Nashville, TN: Upper Room Books, 2001), 14.

2. Elise Eslinger, ed., *Upper Room Worship Book: Music and Liturgies for Spiritual Formation,* (Nashville, TN: Upper Room Books, 2006).

3. Eslinger, ed., *Upper Room Worship Book,* #109.

4. Richard Morgan, *I Never Found that Rocking Chair* (Nashville, TN: Upper Room Books, 1992, #8) o.p.

Made in the USA
Columbia, SC
28 October 2017